# slash your debt

## save money and secure your future

## Gerri Detweiler, Marc Eisenson, & Nancy Castleman

FINANCIAL LITERACY CENTER

BUILDING TRUST THROUGH EDUCATION

Albany, New York

Published by the Financial Literacy Center, Inc.
15 Corporate Circle
Albany, NY 12203
(518) 862-3200

Financial Literacy Center books are available at special quantity discounts to use as premiums and sales promotions, or for use in employee education programs.

**Publisher's Cataloging-in-Publication**
**(Provided by Quality Books, Inc.)**

Detweiler, Gerri.
    Slash your debt : save money and secure your
future. -- 2nd ed.
    p. cm.
    LCCN: 98-76185
    ISBN: 0-9659638-5-3

    1. Finance, Personal. 2. Debt--United States.
3. Consumer credit. I. Eisenson, Marc, 1943-
II. Castleman, Nancy, 1948- III. Title.

HG179.D48 1999           640'.42
                   QBI99-326

# Dedications

*Gerri Detweiler*

For my daughter Sydney, my greatest joy.

*Marc Eisenson*

Dedicated to the Magnificent Seven: Zachary, Joshua, Caitlyn, Andrew, Michael, Eric, and Alison.

*Nancy Castleman*

A million thanks, Marc, for all you teach me and try to teach everyone else.

# Table of Contents

# List of Tables

# Acknowledgments

Between us, we've written and had published three bestselling books. This is the fourth, and it has been a brand-new publishing experience.

Not only did the staff at the Financial Literacy Center (FLC) solicit our thoughts on every aspect of the layout and distribution of *Slash Your Debt,* they really listened to our advice and, unheard of in the publishing industry, actually made changes until everyone was satisfied!

Those of you who have never worked with a publisher may not understand what a deviation this has been from the norm. But let us assure you, this is a great book because of the attitude and cooperation of Shawn Connors and the terrific, dedicated staff he has brought together.

Our many thanks to them all, and also to Linda Spiciarich and Marcy Ross of Good Advice Press, and to our agent Alan Kellock. Their help in bringing this book to life was invaluable.

As much as FLC has changed our perception of the publishing experience, we hope *Slash Your Debt* will change your relationship with money. You have the right to live on less than you earn, without feeling deprived. The secret is debt-free living. The financial freedom that comes with slashing your debt is achievable. You can do it. Thanks to FLC, we believe we can help.

Gerri Detweiler
Marc Eisenson
Nancy Castleman

# Introduction

Sick and tired of facing a stack of bills each month? A debt consolidation loan might be the perfect solution. While you'd still owe as much as you do now, after consolidating your debts, you'd have just one monthly payment and your total interest cost could be reduced. Done right, debt consolidation can save you a fortune, but done wrong, it'll just dig you deeper into debt!

While we know that it's no fun to be mired in debt, and it's often less fun to read "financial" books, we wrote *Slash Your Debt: Save Money and Secure Your Future* to help make your journey to debt-free living as painless as possible. We're about to show you how to successfully consolidate your debts and create the payoff strategy that's right for you. So fasten your seat belt and let's get started slashing those debts!

"*Desperation is sometimes as powerful
an inspirer as genius.*"

– Benjamin Disraeli

# CHAPTER 1

# Debt Consolidation Basics

## The Good News:

- **If you choose the right consolidation loan, you'll have one monthly payment** (or at least fewer payments), which can mean fewer hassles.

- **You can save time and money** — if you choose a debt consolidation loan with an attractive interest rate and reasonable repayment terms.

## The Traps:

- **You may pay *more* with a debt consolidation loan.** That's correct. If you don't choose the right consolidation loan, you can end up forking over even more money than if you had just paid your bills at the higher interest rates.

- **You may be in debt for a very long time.** Some of these loans carry long repayment terms that can keep you in debt for decades, if not generations!

- **You may end up deeper in debt** than when you started. This happens to a lot of folks. Don't let it happen to you! Follow our advice to ensure that you'll get out of debt … and stay out.

Our first goal is to help you choose the lowest-cost debt consolidation option for your situation, which will hopefully mean lowering the interest rate you're being charged. But getting a lower rate is just one of the steps you can take to get out of debt and save a bundle. Another is to pay off your debt as soon as possible, ideally in no more than three to five years.

Throughout this book, we're going to offer many tips that will help you pay off your debts faster, at less cost, and without creating more problems for yourself in the future. Concrete examples will make it easy for you to tune in on the advice that's most relevant to your situation. To keep the numbers as simple as possible, we'll assume your debt is all on one credit card, carrying a 17% interest rate and requiring a minimum monthly payment of 2% of the outstanding balance.

As your balance goes down, so will your required payment. (That's how credit cards work. Mortgages, car loans, student loans, and other personal loans require a predetermined monthly payment that does not get smaller as the balance is paid down.) We'll compare three levels of debt: $5,000, $10,000, and $15,000. If your debt is smaller or larger than that, you'll be able to use the tables we provide for information that more closely matches your situation.

## The Less You're Charged, the More It May Cost

At first glance, it would seem that the lower the interest rate charged on a credit card balance, the less you'll pay in interest. And all things being equal, that would be true. Unfortunately, all things aren't always equal, and the credit card industry has come up with an ingenious way to turn less into more.

If you have a $5,000 balance on your card, and the required minimum payment this month is $150, it might be very tempting to transfer your balance to a card that only requires a $100 monthly payment, and "save" that $50. Credit card issuers promote low, low monthly payments as a way to lure you in. Don't take the bait!

## Minimum Percent Payments

The required monthly payment on a credit card is calculated as a percentage of the outstanding loan balance. Typically ranging from 2% to 3%, the lower the percentage, the less you're required to pay in any one month and the more the debt could cost you over the long run. Assuming a 17% interest rate and a $5,000 balance, a card with a 2% minimum, which is the percent most issuers use these days, would require a $100 payment this month, and it would cost you $11,304 in interest and take you 40 years to pay it off. A 3% card would require a $150 payment this month and would cost $4,296 in interest and 18 years to pay off.

Taking advantage of that 1% lower required payment would cost you $7,008. A pretty lousy deal, we think.

Table #1 shows the numbers for four cards, all with the same balance and interest rate, but different required minimum percent payments.

<table>
<tr><td colspan="5">Table #1</td></tr>
<tr><td colspan="5">What a Difference a Fraction of a Percent Makes</td></tr>
<tr><td colspan="5">Based on a $5,000 credit card balance and a 17% interest rate<br>(For the total outlay, add $5,000 to the interest cost.)</td></tr>
<tr><td>Card</td><td>Minimum % Payment</td><td>First Month's Payment</td><td>Interest Cost</td><td>Years to Payoff</td></tr>
<tr><td>A</td><td>1.67%</td><td>$ 83.50</td><td>$25,354</td><td>81 yrs</td></tr>
<tr><td>B</td><td>2.00</td><td>100.00</td><td>11,304</td><td>40 yrs</td></tr>
<tr><td>C</td><td>2.50</td><td>125.00</td><td>6,210</td><td>24 yrs</td></tr>
<tr><td>D</td><td>3.00</td><td>150.00</td><td>4,296</td><td>18 yrs</td></tr>
</table>

*Note:* These amounts were calculated with *The Banker's Secret Credit Card Software*.

## The Shrinking Monthly Payment

With mortgages, car, and student loans, as well as most other debts, when you sign on the dotted line, you receive a set minimum payment and a set term. For example, on a $100,000, 30-year mortgage at 7%, your principal and interest amount would equal $665.31 per month for 30 years (not including taxes or insurance).

Credit cards don't work that way. Each month, the required payment is calculated based on the new loan balance. As the balance goes down, the required payment goes down as well. With this arrangement, the interest portion of each payment remains large, the part that goes to

| | | Table #2 | | |
|---|---|---|---|---|
| | | **The Shrinking Monthly Payment** | | |
| | | Based on a $5,000 balance on a 17% card with a 2% minimum payment | | |
| Month | Payment Amount | Interest | Principal | Balance |
| 1 | $100.00 | $70.83 | $29.17 | $4,970.83 |
| 2 | 99.42 | 70.42 | 29.00 | 4,941.83 |
| 3 | 98.84 | 70.01 | 28.83 | 4,913.00 |
| 4 | 98.26 | 69.60 | 28.66 | 4,884.34 |
| 5 | 97.69 | 69.19 | 28.50 | 4,855.84 |
| | | | | |
| 100 | 56.03 | 39.69 | 16.34 | 2,785.38 |
| 101 | 55.71 | 39.46 | 16.25 | 2,769.13 |
| 102 | 55.38 | 39.23 | 16.15 | 2,752.98 |
| | | | | |
| 200 | 31.22 | 22.11 | 9.11 | 1,551.66 |
| 201 | 31.03 | 21.98 | 9.05 | 1,542.61 |
| 202 | 30.85 | 21.85 | 9.00 | 1,533.61 |
| | | | | |
| 300 | 17.39 | 12.32 | 5.07 | 864.40 |
| 301 | 17.29 | 12.25 | 5.04 | 859.36 |
| 302 | 17.19 | 12.17 | 5.02 | 854.34 |

*Note:* These amounts were calculated with *The Banker's Secret Credit Card Software*.

the principal portion (the amount you owe) stays small, and the loan goes on and on and on ... .

Table #2 on page 14 shows excerpts from an amortization schedule for a $5,000 credit card bill at 17% with a 2% minimum payment. Note how the monthly payment amount keeps going down, and how little of your payment goes to actually paying off your debt.

## Interest Rate Versus Minimum Payment

The lower the interest rate, we said, the less you'd expect to pay in interest — all things being equal. But all things are rarely equal. A card with a low interest rate combined with a low minimum payment could cost more than a card with a high interest rate and a higher minimum payment. (See Table #3.)

### Table #3
## Secret Credit Card Math
Based on a $5,000 balance

| Card | Interest Rate | Minimum % Payment | Total Interest Cost | Years to Payoff |
|------|---------------|-------------------|---------------------|-----------------|
| A | 13.5% | 1.667% | $9,538 | 41 |
| B | 15.9 | 2.000 | 9,159 | 35 |
| C | 19.8 | 3.000 | 5,858 | 21 |

*Note:* These amounts were calculated with *The Banker's Secret Credit Card Software*.

Now who would have thought that a 19.8% credit card could cost about half as much and take half as long to pay down as a 13.5% card? But that's the way credit card math works! In the above example, the card with the 3% minimum payment is going to cost you far less over the long run than the 2% or 1.667% card.

**KEY POINT** *Here's the bottom line when it comes to credit card bills and, for that matter, to all loans: The more you pay each month, the less you'll pay in total.*

## The Simple but Expensive Truth

Let's say you owe $10,000 on one of your credit cards. The interest rate is 17%, and your monthly minimum payment is calculated as 2% of your outstanding balance. Under this sample scenario, if you don't switch your $10,000 debt to a lower-interest loan, and only send in the required minimum payments, by the time you've paid it off — some 50 years from now (!!!) — you'll have paid back more than three times what you owed: $33,447. The card company will have received $23,447 in interest alone. In other words, every $50 purchase will cost you $167. That's why people who are debt-free or close to it keep getting richer, and why borrowers are always struggling to catch up. Smile. You're about to catch up!

To find out how much you could end up paying if you only send in the minimum required payments on your debts, see Table #4.

| Table #4 | | | | | | | | | | | |
|---|---|---|---|---|---|---|---|---|---|---|---|
| **Only Sending in the Minimum on Your Credit Cards?** | | | | | | | | | | | |
| Here's how much you'll pay and how long it will take to get debt-free. Based on a 2% minimum payment | | | | | | | | | | | |
| | **Interest Rate** | | | | | | | | | | |
| **Loan Balance** | **10%** | **11%** | **12%** | **13%** | **14%** | **15%** | **16%** | **17%** | **18%** | **19%** | **20%** |
| $ 1,000 Outlay | $1,507 | $1,595 | $1,697 | $1,815 | $1,955 | $2,123 | $2,329 | $2,590 | $2,931 | $3,398 | $4,085 |
| Years | 10 | 11 | 11 | 12 | 13 | 14 | 15 | 17 | 19 | 22 | 26 |
| 2,500 Outlay | 4,078 | 4,364 | 4,697 | 5,088 | 5,555 | 6,123 | 6,829 | 7,733 | 8,931 | 10,598 | 13,084 |
| Years | 17 | 17 | 19 | 20 | 22 | 24 | 27 | 30 | 34 | 40 | 49 |
| 5,000 Outlay | 8,364 | 8,979 | 9,697 | 10,542 | 11,555 | 12,789 | 14,329 | 16,304 | 18,931 | 22,598 | 28,085 |
| Years | 22 | 23 | 24 | 26 | 29 | 32 | 35 | 40 | 46 | 54 | 66 |
| 7,500 Outlay | 12,650 | 13,595 | 14,697 | 15,997 | 17,555 | 19,456 | 21,829 | 24,876 | 28,931 | 34,598 | 43,085 |
| Years | 24 | 26 | 28 | 30 | 33 | 36 | 40 | 45 | 52 | 62 | 76 |
| 10,000 Outlay | 16,935 | 18,211 | 19,696 | 21,451 | 23,555 | 26,123 | 29,329 | *33,447* | 38,931 | 46,597 | 58,084 |
| Years | 26 | 28 | 30 | 33 | 36 | 39 | 44 | *50* | 57 | 68 | 83 |
| 15,000 Outlay | 25,507 | 27,441 | 29,697 | 32,361 | 35,555 | 39,456 | 44,330 | 50,590 | 58,932 | 70,598 | 88,084 |
| Years | 29 | 31 | 34 | 36 | 40 | 44 | 49 | 55 | 64 | 76 | 94 |
| 20,000 Outlay | 34,078 | 36,672 | 39,697 | 43,270 | 47,555 | 52,790 | 59,330 | 67,733 | 78,931 | 94,598 | 118,083 |
| Years | 31 | 33 | 36 | 39 | 43 | 47 | 52 | 59 | 69 | 82 | 101 |
| 25,000 Outlay | 42,649 | 45,903 | 49,697 | 54,179 | 59,555 | 66,123 | 74,330 | 84,875 | 98,931 | 118,598 | 148,084 |
| Years | 33 | 35 | 38 | 41 | 45 | 49 | 55 | 63 | 72 | 86 | 106 |
| 30,000 Outlay | 51,221 | 55,133 | 59,696 | 65,088 | 71,555 | 79,456 | 89,329 | 102,019 | 118,931 | 142,599 | 178,085 |
| Years | 34 | 37 | 39 | 43 | 47 | 51 | 58 | 65 | 75 | 90 | 111 |

Note: These amounts were calculated with *The Banker's Secret Credit Card Software*.

If you're feeling overwhelmed, upset, or angry about your financial situation, you aren't alone. Millions of people face these kinds of challenges each year. But once you take charge of your debts, you're going to experience an incredible sense of accomplishment that will benefit you and your family for the rest of your lives.

You can do it! These eight key steps will help you win your war against debt.

## 1. Shop, shop, shop.

In the following three chapters, we'll describe numerous, specific debt consolidation loan options. Take the time to shop around and choose carefully. The money you save will be your own!

When you shop for clothing or other merchandise, you compare the price tag, and hopefully the quality, as well as the reliability of the manufacturer and merchant. When you shop for a debt consolidation loan, you have to compare the Annual Percentage Rate (APR) — and the total payback time. Why? Some loans can take as little as three years to pay off, others 10 or more. The longer the term, the more you'll pay ... even if the interest rate is exactly the same. To make an accurate comparison of your total costs, you'll want to know exactly how much you'll pay the lender over the entire loan period. If the lender doesn't give you the total cost of the loan, we'll show you how to figure it out.

## 2. Know thyself.

Be honest about why you got into debt in the first place, and realize that getting out of debt may well require changes in your habits and lifestyle. Don't look at these changes as "punishment." Instead, use this time as a learning opportunity to take control of your financial future. In Chapter 9 we'll give you strategies for cutting costs, handling emergencies, and setting up a spending plan that works.

If you follow our advice, your debts will not cost you nearly as much as you might have thought when you looked at Table #4 on page 16. You'll have more money to spend on those people and things that really matter to you. And a great stress will be gone from your life — hopefully forever.

### 3. Have a plan.

Research by the Consumer Federation of America and NationsBank has shown that people with incomes between $10,000 and $100,000 who say they have a written financial plan report twice as much money in savings and investments as people without a plan. Similarly, you're much more likely to succeed if you have a plan for consolidating and paying off your debts. Using Table #5 on page 20, you'll be able to create a plan for paying back the money you owe in three to five years at most.

### 4. Save money.

It may sound obvious, but don't consolidate using a loan with a higher interest rate. For example, don't use a consolidation loan at 14% to pay off a student loan charging 8%, even if that means you'll only have one monthly payment rather than multiple bills to juggle.

### 5. Start high, work down.

If you can't qualify for enough credit to consolidate all your bills, consolidate the ones with the highest interest rates first.

### 6. Ask!

Don't be afraid to negotiate for a lower interest rate or fees. You may be able to get a discount if you are already a customer of the bank or credit union, if you are willing to bring your other accounts there, and/or if you let your payments be automatically deducted from your account. Remember, not asking is an automatic "No!"

### 7. Know the rules.

If you are unable to pay back a loan, but successfully negotiate a reduced payback (perhaps to avoid bankruptcy), there may be tax consequences. The IRS considers "forgiveness of a loan" a taxable activity and Uncle Sam may want to take his share of the discount as if it were income to you.

### 8. Be realistic.

Understand that debt consolidation is just one tactic in what will be your overall strategy to get out of debt. Consolidation won't make your debts magically disappear, but it can help you get a handle on them if you use it in the right way.

## It's Time to Consolidate

Hopefully, seeing in black and white just how much those credit cards could cost you will motivate you to do something — in fact, probably many things — to get out of debt.

Now take a look at Table #5 on page 20. It shows you how little you'll need to send in, after you've consolidated, to pay off your debts in three to five years rather than in a few decades. You'll probably be surprised!

Perhaps the greatest motivator of all will be to see how much you can save by consolidating your debts and paying them off in three to five years. Table #6 on page 21 will show you.

## Table #5

## After You've Consolidated — Pick a Monthly Payment to Pay Your Debt Off in Three to Five Years

| Debt | Years | Consolidation Loan Rate | | | | | | |
|---|---|---|---|---|---|---|---|---|
| | | 8% | 9% | 10% | 11% | 12% | 13% | 14% |
| $ 5,000 | 3 | $ 157 | $ 159 | $ 161 | $ 164 | $ 166 | $ 168 | $ 171 |
| | 5 | 101 | 104 | 106 | 109 | 111 | 114 | 116 |
| 7,500 | 3 | 235 | 239 | 242 | 246 | 249 | 253 | 256 |
| | 5 | 152 | 156 | 159 | 163 | 167 | 171 | 175 |
| 10,000 | 3 | 313 | 318 | 323 | 327 | 332 | 337 | 342 |
| | 5 | 203 | 208 | 212 | 217 | 222 | 228 | 233 |
| 12,500 | 3 | 392 | 398 | 403 | 409 | 415 | 421 | 427 |
| | 5 | 253 | 259 | 266 | 272 | 278 | 284 | 291 |
| 15,000 | 3 | 470 | 477 | 484 | 491 | 498 | 505 | 513 |
| | 5 | 304 | 311 | 319 | 326 | 334 | 341 | 349 |
| 17,500 | 3 | 548 | 557 | 565 | 573 | 581 | 590 | 598 |
| | 5 | 355 | 363 | 372 | 381 | 389 | 398 | 407 |
| 20,000 | 3 | 627 | 636 | 645 | 655 | 664 | 674 | 684 |
| | 5 | 406 | 415 | 425 | 435 | 445 | 455 | 465 |
| 25,000 | 3 | 783 | 795 | 807 | 818 | 830 | 842 | 854 |
| | 5 | 507 | 519 | 531 | 544 | 556 | 569 | 582 |
| 30,000 | 3 | 940 | 954 | 968 | 982 | 996 | 1,011 | 1,025 |
| | 5 | 608 | 623 | 637 | 652 | 667 | 683 | 698 |
| 35,000 | 3 | 1,097 | 1,113 | 1,129 | 1,146 | 1,163 | 1,179 | 1,196 |
| | 5 | 710 | 727 | 744 | 761 | 779 | 796 | 814 |
| 40,000 | 3 | 1,253 | 1,272 | 1,291 | 1,310 | 1,329 | 1,348 | 1,367 |
| | 5 | 811 | 830 | 850 | 870 | 890 | 910 | 931 |
| 45,000 | 3 | 1,410 | 1,431 | 1,452 | 1,473 | 1,495 | 1,516 | 1,538 |
| | 5 | 912 | 934 | 956 | 978 | 1,001 | 1,024 | 1,047 |
| 50,000 | 3 | 1,567 | 1,590 | 1,613 | 1,637 | 1,661 | 1,685 | 1,709 |
| | 5 | 1,014 | 1,038 | 1,062 | 1,087 | 1,112 | 1,138 | 1,163 |

Note: These amounts, calculated using The Banker's Secret Loan Software, will help you save a bundle on your debts. To save the most, first consolidate to get the lowest interest rate you can. Then pay your debt off as fast as you can — preferably in three to five years.

## Table #6

# After You've Consolidated — How Much Can You Save?

Based on a $10,000 credit card balance
with a 2% minimum required payment

| Card Interest | 13% | 14% | 15% | 16% | 17% | 18% | 19% |
|---|---|---|---|---|---|---|---|
| Total Card Cost | $21,451 | 23,555 | 26,123 | 29,329 | 33,447 | 38,931 | 46,598 |

| Consolidation Loan | | Amount Saved by Consolidating | | | | | | |
|---|---|---|---|---|---|---|---|---|
| Interest | Years | | | | | | | |
| 8% | 3 | $10,170 | $12,274 | $14,842 | $18,048 | $22,166 | $27,650 | $35,317 |
| | 5 | 9,285 | 11,389 | 13,957 | 17,163 | 21,281 | 26,765 | 34,432 |
| 9% | 3 | 10,003 | 12,107 | 14,675 | 17,881 | 21,999 | 27,483 | 35,150 |
| | 5 | 8,996 | 11,100 | 13,668 | 16,874 | 20,992 | 26,476 | 34,143 |
| 10% | 3 | 9,835 | 11,939 | 14,507 | 17,713 | 21,831 | 27,315 | 34,982 |
| | 5 | 8,703 | 10,807 | 13,375 | 16,581 | 20,699 | 26,183 | 33,850 |
| 11% | 3 | 9,665 | 11,769 | 14,337 | 17,543 | 21,661 | 27,145 | 34,812 |
| | 5 | 8,406 | 10,510 | 13,078 | 16,284 | 20,402 | 25,886 | 33,553 |
| 12% | 3 | 9,494 | 11,598 | 14,166 | 17,372 | 21,490 | 26,974 | 34,641 |
| | 5 | 8,104 | 10,208 | 12,776 | 15,982 | 20,100 | 25,584 | 33,251 |
| 13% | 3 | 9,321 | 11,425 | 13,993 | 17,199 | 21,317 | 26,801 | 34,468 |
| | 5 | 7,799 | 9,903 | 12,471 | 15,677 | 19,795 | 25,279 | 32,946 |
| 14% | 3 | 9,147 | 11,251 | 13,819 | 17,025 | 21,143 | 26,627 | 34,294 |
| | 5 | 7,490 | 9,594 | 12,162 | 15,368 | 19,486 | 24,970 | 32,637 |
| 15% | 3 | 8,972 | 11,076 | 13,644 | 16,850 | 20,968 | 26,452 | 34,118 |
| | 5 | 7,177 | 9,281 | 11,849 | 15,055 | 19,173 | 24,657 | 32,324 |
| 16% | 3 | 8,795 | 10,899 | 13,467 | 16,673 | 20,791 | 26,275 | 33,942 |
| | 5 | 6,860 | 8,964 | 11,532 | 14,738 | 18,856 | 24,340 | 32,007 |
| 17% | 3 | 8,616 | 10,720 | 13,288 | 16,494 | 20,612 | 26,096 | 33,763 |
| | 5 | 6,540 | 8,644 | 11,212 | 14,418 | 18,536 | 24,020 | 31,687 |
| 18% | 3 | 8,436 | 10,540 | 13,108 | 16,314 | 20,432 | 25,916 | 33,583 |
| | 5 | 6,215 | 8,319 | 10,887 | 14,093 | 18,211 | 23,695 | 31,362 |

**How to use this chart:** Say you owe $10,000 at 17%. If you only send in the minimum, you'll spend **$33,447**.

But if you get a lower interest rate — 11%, for example — and pay it off in five years, you'll save **$20,402**. These amounts were calculated with *The Banker's Secret Loan Software*.

"One pays for everything, the trick is not
to pay too much of anything for anything."

– John Steinbeck

# CHAPTER 2

# Unsecured Loans

When most of us think about debt consolidation, we picture asking a banker or credit union officer for a loan to pay off our other bills. This type of loan is called an "unsecured" loan because it doesn't require any collateral, like a car or a home, to back it up. In addition to working with your local bank or credit union, you may also be able to get an unsecured loan from friends, family members, or even from a credit card company. (Yes, when you charge on your credit card, you're taking out an unsecured loan!)

Lenders consider unsecured loans to be the most risky — because all they have from you is your signature. There's no house or car to "secure" the loan, that is, to be foreclosed or repossessed if you don't pay what you owe. Because these loans are considered riskier, lenders generally charge higher rates and fees than they would for secured loans, like mortgages. And unsecured loans are typically more difficult to obtain than secured loans, especially if you have a lot of debt.

On the other hand, the money lending business, especially credit card lending, is very competitive these days, so you may have many more options than you realize. In this chapter, we'll describe three kinds of unsecured loans, and we'll tell you how to use each of them to your advantage:

- personal loans
- credit card "loans"
- loans from family and friends

## Personal Loans

Personal loans from banks, credit unions, and finance companies give you the opportunity to consolidate some or all of your other bills into one loan with a fixed monthly payment and a fixed repayment period, usually three to five years.

## The Good News:

The typical unsecured personal loan must be paid off in three to five years, which holds you to a forced payoff schedule instead of letting you stretch your payments over decades, as often happens with credit cards. And if you can get an attractive interest rate, a debt consolidation loan can save you a lot of money by lowering your interest cost.

## The Bad News:

There's a good reason why it can be difficult to get a loan when you most need one. Even though your intention may be to pay off your other bills with the new loan, if you have substantial debts, lenders may fear that you're really looking to get deeper into debt, not to get out of it. When considering your application, they may add your current monthly debt payments to the payment that would be required on the new loan, and turn you down because your debt load is too high.

Unsecured loans often carry higher interest rates than secured loans. Again, that's because there's no collateral — nothing for the lender to repossess or foreclose and sell. Interest rates on personal loans generally range from a low of 8.25% to 18%, with the average as of this writing at around 13% to 14%.

## Success Strategies:

- **Pay attention to the total cost of the loan.** Sales pitches for these loans often focus on the "low monthly payment," not on the interest rate, term, or total cost.

  **⊶ KEY POINT** *A low monthly payment with a high interest rate and/or a long repayment plan will make it very expensive to pay the debt off, and can actually put you deeper in the hole.*

- **Negotiate!** If you've been a long-time customer at a bank, for example, and are willing to have your payments deducted directly from your checking account, or have found a better deal somewhere else, ask for a break on the interest rate.

## Where to Shop:

A consolidation loan is a major financial commitment, so always call at least three lenders to find out what they have to offer. Your local newspaper may have already done the legwork for you. Many list the rates at area lenders at least once a week.

The BanxQuote Web site (www.banx.com) lists current rates on unsecured personal loans at banks in each region of the United States. If you have access to the Internet, this is another way to check out rates in your area.

If you belong to a credit union, it may offer a good deal. If you don't belong to a credit union, you may be eligible for membership in one. To find out, send a self-addressed, stamped envelope to:

Credit Union National Association
P.O. Box 431
Madison, WI 53701

Or check out its Web site at: www.cuna.org. For a sampling of credit union interest rates around the United States, go to www.bankrate.com.

## Watch Out For:

**High-rate loans.** Usually offered by finance companies, we've seen rates as high as 25% and more! Don't even consider them.

**Bill-paying services and advance-fee loans.** These companies promise to help you get out of debt, but are more likely to make your situation worse. See Chapter 8.

## How Much You Can Save:

**If you transfer your balance to a personal loan at 14% for three to five years ...**

> **If you have a $5,000 credit card balance at 17%**
> **Pay it off in 3 years: You'll save $10,152**
> **Pay it off in 5 years: You'll save $9,324**
>
> **If you have a $10,000 balance at 17%**
> **Pay it off in 3 years: You'll save $21,143**
> **Pay it off in 5 years: You'll save $19,486**
>
> **If you have a $15,000 balance at 17%**
> **Pay it off in 3 years: You'll save $32,134**
> **Pay it off in 5 years: You'll save $29,649**

### Credit Card "Loans"

Credit cards can actually be used as great consolidation loans. By transferring the outstanding balance on a higher-rate card (or loan) to one with a lower rate, you can save a considerable amount in interest.

Most issuers make it very easy to transfer balances from one card to another, by offering "convenience checks." These checks look just like personal checks, and cardholders are encouraged to use them to pay off higher-interest debts.

## The Good News:

If you have a good, strong credit history, you may qualify for a credit card with a much lower rate than you could get on a typical unsecured consolidation loan. And the application may already be waiting in your mailbox! Card issuers have been sending out more than 3 billion solicitations every year. You might receive a pre-approved offer today or tomorrow, for a card that starts with a rate of 5.9%, or even less, typically for three to six months. Competition between lenders is fierce, and if you have a good credit rating, the proof will be sent to you in the mail.

## The Bad News:

Some card issuers charge higher interest rates and/or special fees for convenience checks or balance transfers, which can make this option more expensive than it may seem. Ask about the interest rate and any fees, and figure them into your total cost before you transfer debts to a new credit card.

In addition, since the required payments on credit cards get smaller and smaller every month (assuming you don't charge anything else on the card), you may be tempted to send in less and less as time goes on, stretching out your debt for decades. Be sure to send in enough every month to pay the debt off in three to five years. Table #5 on page 20 will show you how much that amount should be.

## Success Strategies:

- **Use what you've got.** First, take a look in your wallet. A great rate may be waiting right there! Call your current issuers and tell them you'd like to transfer some of your other credit card debt to their card — but only if they can give you a competitive rate. Be persistent. If the customer service representative can't help, ask to speak to a supervisor. Chances are at least one will bite.

    Then, if you don't have enough credit available, ask for a credit line increase. If you've been paying your bills on time, most credit card companies will be happy to give you more credit. After all, that's how they make their money!

- **Low but steady often wins.** While you can save more by strategically transferring your debt to another low introductory-rate card whenever the last "teaser" rate is about to expire, the constant balance swapping could burn you out. If that's your case, take the time to sift through the offers and find one with a steady, low interest rate.

- **Have a plan.** Once you've consolidated, stop charging and create a plan for paying off the debt as quickly as possible. Consider asking the card issuer, your bank, or your credit union to transfer a fixed payment each month, or even twice a month, from your bank account to your credit card issuer. That way, you won't be tempted to pay less or to take advantage of a "skip payment" offer.

## Where to Shop:

In addition to carefully evaluating the offers that are mailed to you, comprehensive lists of low-rate cards are available at www.cardtrak.com.

Or send $5 to:
CardTrak
P.O. Box 1700
Frederick, MD 21702

For a free (but less frequently updated) list, send an SASE with 55¢ postage to:
Consumer Action — Low-Rate List
717 Market Street, Suite 310
San Francisco, CA 94103

## Do-It-Yourself Payoff Plans

If you'd like to create your own personalized payoff plan and are interested in tools we have created to make this easy, see page 87.

## Watch Out For:

**Expensive fees.** It doesn't hurt to ask the card issuer to waive a transfer fee or cash advance fee *before* you transfer your balance. Issuers want your business, and they want to give you all the credit you can handle (and sometimes more) because that's "where the money is" for them.

**Higher interest rates.** Make sure you won't end up paying more for transfers than you expected. Sometimes the advertised interest rate is only for purchases. You have to specifically ask what the rate will be for a transfer.

**Teaser rates.** Very low to start, these rates may jump dramatically after a few months. You can use the initial low rate to your advantage, but may be better off basing your decision about whether or not to transfer on the longer-term rate — unless you're sure you'll be able to get a new card with a teaser rate and you'll remember to make the transfer before the rate skyrockets.

## How Much You Can Save:

If you transfer your balance to a teaser card with a rate of 5.9% —
and keep transferring the balance for three to five years ...

> **If you have a $5,000 credit card balance at 17%**
> Pay it off in 3 years: You'll save $10,836
> Pay it off in 5 years: You'll save $10,518

> **If you have a $10,000 balance at 17%**
> Pay it off in 3 years: You'll save $22,512
> Pay it off in 5 years: You'll save $21,875

> **If you have a $15,000 balance at 17%**
> Pay it off in 3 years: You'll save $34,187
> Pay it off in 5 years: You'll save $33,232

## Loans From Family and Friends

Loans from family and friends can be among the most helpful — and the most dangerous.

### The Good News:

You may be able to create a "win-win" situation — if you can offer the "lenders" (for example, your parents) an interest rate that's less than you would have to pay a financial institution, and more than they are currently earning. If the loan is appropriately recorded as a second mortgage on your home, you may even be able to deduct the interest, just as you would on a home equity loan from a bank. (Check with your tax advisor or lawyer. Not everyone qualifies for the home equity loan tax break.)

### The Bad News:

You may end up destroying your relationships if you are unable to repay the loan. Before borrowing, make sure that all involved are agreeable. If you plan to borrow from your sister, for example, you may want to be certain that her spouse also agrees to the loan, or you may both be put into an uncomfortable position. And if Mom and Dad lend you the money at a below-market interest rate, the IRS may very well expect them to pay taxes on the interest you would have had to pay a bank! Also, if you are unable to pay back the loan, there may be tax consequences. The IRS considers "forgiveness of a loan" a taxable activity and may want to take its share from you.

## Success Strategies:

- **Treat it like a serious loan.** Approach family and friends with a specific plan, including the interest rate you will pay them and how much you'll repay each month. Table #5 on page 20 will give you the numbers.

  Insist on putting the agreement in writing, so you won't be tempted to put that bill low on your priority list. Propose late charges if you miss payments by more than a certain amount of time, and have a plan for what will happen if you default on the loan. Is there anything you can put up as collateral? Pay off the loan early, and you'll be on their list of preferred borrowers should a future need arise.

- **Make yourself pay.** Ask if the bank will automatically transfer the monthly payment from your account to theirs. (Your financial institution may be willing to create a payoff schedule for you, or we can. See page 87.)

  *Note to parents:* If your children approach you for a loan, think *seriously* before agreeing. If you do decide to lend money, keep it on a professional level (e.g., put it in writing), and your offspring will learn how the real world of borrowing works.

## Watch Out For:

**Pressuring loved ones for the loan.** Even if you feel desperate, back off if your brother or best friend seems uncomfortable. If you can't make your payments, it's better to deal with a bank or credit union than a friend or relative. The emotional cost of defaulting on a loan from friends and relatives can be very, very high.

# How Much You Can Save:

If you borrow from family or friends at 8% ...

> If you have a $5,000 credit card balance at 17%
> Pay it off in 3 years: You'll save $10,664
> Pay it off in 5 years: You'll save $10,221
>
> If you have a $10,000 balance at 17%
> Pay it off in 3 years: You'll save $22,166
> Pay it off in 5 years: You'll save $21,281
>
> If you have a $15,000 balance at 17%
> Pay it off in 3 years: You'll save $33,668
> Pay it off in 5 years: You'll save $32,341

" 'Tis not knowing much, but what is useful,
that makes a wise man."

– Thomas Fuller, M.D.

# CHAPTER 3

# Putting It on the House

**Home Equity Loans**

W ell over a third of all home equity loans are used for debt consolidation. It's the single biggest reason cited for taking such a loan.

With a home equity loan, you can borrow against the current value of your home, minus any first mortgage. It used to be that the typical home equity loan allowed you to borrow up to 80% of the value of your house, less the first mortgage. But now, a new type of home equity loan allows you to borrow more than your house is worth — up to 125% of its value — minus any first mortgage.

There are generally two kinds of home equity loans. The first, also known as a second mortgage, lets you borrow a fixed amount of money for a fixed period of time, often 10 or 15 years. (The interest rate is usually fixed too, but not always.)

The second, a home equity line of credit, allows you to borrow up to a pre-approved credit limit. The repayment period can be much longer on lines of credit — up to 20 years — and the interest rate is often variable.

## The Good News:

Home equity loans often offer attractive rates and the interest *may* be tax deductible as long as the amount you borrow doesn't exceed the difference between the fair market value of your home and the balance of your first mortgage, up to a maximum of $100,000. Married people filing separately are only allowed to deduct interest on a loan of up to $50,000.

## The Bad News:

Even if you're a homeowner with lots of equity in your house, unless you have a strong credit history and steady, verifiable income, you will probably pay a higher interest rate on a home equity loan than the advertised rates. And home equity loans often come with very expensive fees and closing costs.

Because you are putting your house on the line, your risk is a lot greater than with an unsecured loan, like a credit card, where there is no collateral involved. If you can't pay your credit card bills, the card issuer can't take your house. But if you borrow against your house to consolidate debts and then can't pay your home equity loan, foreclosure is a real possibility.

**KEY POINT** *The newer 125% loans, which allow you to borrow more than the value of your home, can be particularly risky.*

Even if you feel confident about your ability to make the payments, what would happen if you had to move? It's highly unlikely that you would be able to sell your house for more than its current value. In some parts of the country, you'd be lucky to get 100% of what you paid. Then you'd have to find another lender willing to loan you the difference between the 125% loan amount and what you got from the sale of the house — which could be difficult at best.

Also, please note that you cannot deduct interest on any part of a home equity loan that exceeds the fair market value of your home. The IRS has said it is monitoring the 125% loans carefully to make sure that consumers aren't incorrectly trying to write off the nondeductible interest.

## The Tax Deduction Myth

Paying interest on a home equity loan or a mortgage is tax deductible ... some of the time. There's a myth that paying mortgage interest will save you lots of money. Not so! It may save you some money and it may save you none, but you never get back more from the IRS than you sent to your lender.

Whether you rent or buy, whether you pay mortgage interest or not, Uncle Sam gives us each a standard deduction. For 2001 that is a $7,600 deduction for couples and a $4,550 deduction for singles.

That means you don't save a nickel in taxes unless you can itemize more than that $7,600 (for couples). For example, if your itemized deductions for 2001 are $10,000, and you're in a 15% tax bracket, your tax benefit will NOT be 15% of $10,000 ($1,500). It will be 15% of $2,400 (the difference between $10,000 and $7,600), — only $360.

## Success Strategies:

- **Have a realistic plan** in place for changing your spending habits before you consolidate with a home equity loan. Of all the consolidation options, the home equity option probably carries the greatest risk. For that reason, you absolutely must be able to change your spending habits. To be sure you can, before applying for an equity loan, practice living on a lower income and saving the difference.

- **Stop taking on new debt!** Avoid taking on additional debt until the home equity loan is paid in full. It is very easy, once you have consolidated using one of these loans, to feel like you have some "breathing room." Pretty soon, out come the credit cards, and before too long, you're even deeper in debt. Don't let this happen to you!

## Table #7

# Pay Off Your Home Equity Loan as Fast as You Can

The cost of a 9% home equity loan if paid off in 3 years, 5 years, 10 years, or 15 years

| Amount | Term | Required Payment | Interest Cost | Total Payment |
|---|---|---|---|---|
| $5,000 | 3 Years | $159 | $ 724 | $ 5,724 |
| | 5 Years | 104 | 1,227 | 6,227 |
| | 10 Years | 63 | 2,600 | 7,600 |
| | 15 Years | 51 | 4,127 | 9,127 |
| $10,000 | 3 Years | 318 | 1,448 | 11,448 |
| | 5 Years | 208 | 2,455 | 12,455 |
| | 10 Years | 127 | 5,201 | 15,201 |
| | 15 Years | 101 | 8,256 | 18,256 |
| $15,000 | 3 Years | 477 | 2,172 | 17,172 |
| | 5 Years | 311 | 3,682 | 18,682 |
| | 10 Years | 190 | 7,801 | 22,801 |
| | 15 Years | 152 | 12,385 | 27,385 |

*Note:* The above numbers were calculated with *The Banker's Secret Loan Software*, and do not include closing costs — which can be considerable.

- **Choose a short repayment period.** Even with a low interest rate and a tax break here or there, you'll end up paying a pretty penny by the time you're through paying off a 10- or 15-year consolidation loan.

  Even if you agree to a longer repayment period, pre-pay your loan, so that in three to five years, you'll be in the clear. In Chapter 7, we'll show you exactly how to do it.

- **Avoid loans for more than the value of your home.** You can't deduct all of the interest, you're putting your house at risk, and the costs on these loans are extremely high. Although they are often advertised with low rates, the effective interest rate can be 25% or more when closing costs are figured in! At that rate, you'll never get out of debt. Our advice? Just say, "NO!"

SLASH YOUR DEBT: Save Money and Secure Your Future

## Where to Shop:

Call local banks and credit unions for information on home equity loans. HSH Associates also offers an informative booklet, *Home Equity: A Consumer's Guide to Loans and Lines*. Send $3 to:

HSH Associates
1200 Route 23
Butler, NJ 07405

Also, visit its Web site at: www.hsh.com for a listing of current home equity rates in major cities across the country.

## Watch Out For:

**High closing costs,** including application fees, appraisal fees, recording fees, title insurance fees, attorney fees, and points. These can total as much as $5,000 on a $25,000 loan! Ask which fees can be waived, and don't pay application fees unless they will be refunded if you are not approved.

**Low introductory rates.** After six months to a year, they'll jump up — raising your interest cost, just as they would on a credit card with a teaser rate.

**Offers for more plastic.** Think twice (or more) before accepting a credit card tied to your home equity line of credit. They make it awfully easy to charge, and your goal should be to get out of debt, not more deeply into it.

## How Much You Can Save:

If you transfer your balance to a 9% home equity loan ...

> **If you have a $5,000 credit card balance at 17%**
> Pay it off in 3 years: You'll save $10,580
> Pay it off in 5 years: You'll save $10,077

> **If you have a $10,000 balance at 17%**
> Pay it off in 3 years: You'll save $21,999
> Pay it off in 5 years: You'll save $20,992

> **If you have a $15,000 balance at 17%**
> Pay it off in 3 years: You'll save $33,418
> Pay it off in 5 years: You'll save $31,908

## Refinancing Your Mortgage

Home equity loans aren't the only way to tap your house for cash to pay off high-interest debts. Your first mortgage can be a great debt consolidation tool, if you're a candidate for a "refi." (That's bank lingo for refinancing your mortgage.)

How can you fit this bill? In either of two ways:

1. If your mortgage represents a relatively small portion of your home equity.

2. If you're paying a higher interest rate on your mortgage than the current rates being charged.

To use a refi as a debt consolidation tool, you'd refinance the outstanding balance on your existing mortgage plus an additional amount sufficient to pay off your higher-interest debts. Let's say you're seven years into a $100,000, 30-year mortgage at 8.5% and have a $93,078 balance (monthly payment: $769), and you also have $20,000 worth of high-interest credit card debt (current month's payment: $400). Assuming the property value has appreciated slightly, you might be able to refinance the existing mortgage at 7% and borrow an additional $20,000, plus enough to cover the closing costs, for a total of $115,000. (See page 40.)

## The Good News:

For about the same mortgage payment you've been making each month — or less — you'll be able to pay off your high-interest debts in one fell swoop. Refinancing $115,000 for 30 years at 7% would mean monthly payments of $765. And this interest would be tax deductible.

## The Bad News:

If you refinance at 7% and take the full 30 years to pay off your new home mortgage, your total cost would be almost the same as if you just continued paying on the current mortgage and credit card bills — but your home would be at increased jeopardy. Why? Because you would be borrowing against more of your home equity for a longer period of time.

So be sure to follow the Success Strategies we list below to whittle down that term! But don't be talked into taking out a 15-year mortgage, unless you're *sure* you'll have no problem with the higher monthly payments.

You don't want to jeopardize your home ownership should the you-know-what hit the you-know-where. You'd be better off taking out a 30-year loan and paying it off in 15 years or less, as your finances allow. (See page 41 for more on this subject.)

*Note:* If you're self-employed or have less than perfect credit, you probably won't qualify for the best available rates, and your costs will be greater.

## Success Strategies:

- **Keep making the same monthly payments.** Let's say that in addition to your mortgage payments, you've been paying $400 toward other debts. Stop charging and put all that toward your refinanced mortgage. Rather than spending $279,944, you'll spend only $171,434, and be free and clear in 12 years and three months. That's a savings of $108,510!

- **Negotiate everything.** Points and fees are negotiable, especially if lenders are hungry for customers. Check rates, points, and fees with at least three to five lenders before you make a decision.

- **Pay closing costs outright.** If you have the cash available, pay the closing costs upfront instead of folding them into the new loan. You'll save a nice chunk of change on interest charges over the life of the loan.

Table #8

# To Save the Most, Refinance and Pre-Pay

### Based on $20,000 credit card and $93,078 mortgage balances

Total cost of current debts without refinancing: **$279,944**
Amount to be saved by refinancing: **$ 4,510**
Amount to be saved by refinancing and pre-paying: **$108,510**

| | | Amount Owed | Required Payment | Interest Rate | Time to Payoff | Payment | Total Payment | Savings |
|---|---|---|---|---|---|---|---|---|
| Current Debts | Mortgage Credit Card | $93,078 $20,000 | $769 $400[1] | 8.5% 17% | 23 Yrs 60 Yrs | $212,211 $67,733 | $279,944 | $0 |
| After Refinancing | Mortgage Credit Card | $115,000[2] — | $765 — | 7% — | 30 Yrs — | $275,434 — | $275,434 | $4,510[4] |
| After Refinancing and Pre-Paying [3] | Mortgage Credit Card | $115,000[2] — | $1,169[3] — | 7% — | 12 Yrs/ 3 Mths — | $171,434 — | $171,434 | $108,510 |

Notes:

1. Assuming a 17% credit card that requires a 2% minimum payment, $400 would be the required payment this month. The required payment would go down every month as the balance goes down.

2. This includes the $93,078 mortgage balance, the $20,000 credit card debt, as well as closing costs.

3. Here, we're assuming that you would be paying the same amount each month as you're required to send in this month on the mortgage and credit card bill — $769 + $400 = $1,169.

4. Savings do not include tax savings from additional deductible mortgage interest.

The above numbers were calculated with *The Banker's Secret Loan and Credit Card Software*.

# Where to Shop:

Contact local banks, mortgage brokers, and credit unions. Ask friends and neighbors for recommendations.

For our advice on how to compare loan options, read "Buying the Right Mortgage — New or Refinanced" in *Invest in Yourself: Six Secrets to a Rich Life* (see page 107).

Visit HSH Associates' Web site at: www.hsh.com for a listing of current mortgage rates in major cities across the country.

# Watch Out For:

**High closing costs.** As with home equity loans, lenders can come up with a pile of expensive fees. Always try to get the fees waived or reduced.

**Slacking off your payment regimen.** If you don't keep making extra payments on your refinanced mortgage, you'll get hit with big interest costs over the life of the loan. For example, on the refi we've been discussing, making only the required monthly principal and interest payment of $765 means that the total interest on the new loan amount would be $160,434. With pre-payments of an additional $404 a month (the total $1,169 payment required this month on both your credit card bill and your mortgage), the new loan's interest would be just $56,434. If you don't trust yourself to plow the money into your mortgage, arrange a direct transfer of the additional amount from your checking account.

**Committing to a shorter term.** We absolutely want to see you get out of debt as soon as possible. But we don't encourage you to refinance to a 15-year mortgage. Why? Once you sign on the dotted line for a 15-year mortgage, you're committed to those monthly payments year in and year out — in good times and bad. We wish you nothing but good times, and hope that you'll have the cash to keep up with those bigger payments each month. But in case times get tough, a 30-year mortgage will give you breathing room. Take out the 30-year loan, then pay if off in 15 years ... or less.

"It requires a great deal of boldness and
a great deal of caution to make a great
fortune, and when you have got it,
it requires ten times as much wit to keep it."

– Ralph Waldo Emerson

# CHAPTER 4

# When You're Your Own Lender

**Retirement Loans**

I f you *withdraw* money from your retirement account before your official retirement age, you'll be hit with penalties and taxes. *Borrowing* from the account instead will let you pay off your higher-interest debts, without paying penalties or fees — if you do it correctly.

In most cases, you can borrow funds from your 401(k), 403(b), or profit-sharing plan — usually up to 50% of your account, to a maximum of $50,000, generally at 1% or 2% above the prime interest rate. For example, if prime is 8%, you would pay somewhere between 9% and 10%. (The prime rate is published in the financial pages of many newspapers, or visit www.bankrate.com.)

The IRS requires you to pay back this type of loan in roughly equal monthly installments over five years, unless the loan is used to purchase a home. As long as the home is to be your principal residence, the loan can be for more than a five-year term. (Table #5 on page 20 will help you determine the correct amount for a three- or five-year payback.)

IRA funds are the exception. You can use money from your IRA interest-free, but — and it's a big "but" — you must "roll it over" to another IRA account within 60 days. Don't use your IRA to pay debts unless you are *100% confident* the money will be replaced within two months, say, with a commission check you are guaranteed to receive. Otherwise, you'll be hit with a penalty and taxes on the funds. (Of course, while you're using your IRA money, it won't be earning you any interest.)

## The Good News:

For people with no credit history or a poor credit history, loans against a retirement plan can be a godsend, because they are typically very easy to get. There's no credit check, and no credit application is required. In addition, they charge low rates, and the interest you pay is credited back to your account, so you are paying interest to yourself, as opposed to a bank or other lender.

## The Bad News:

You may very well end up robbing your retirement fund if you rely too much on these loans. First, you will not be earning anything on that portion of your retirement account you've borrowed. Sure, you'll be paying interest to yourself, but paying interest to yours truly and earning a return on your money from someone else are two different things altogether. Plus, the interest you pay yourself on the loan may be less than you can make on some retirement plan investment options. And that would mean less money when you retire.

There's another big danger: If you don't make your payments as required, the IRS will treat your loan as a withdrawal, which means you'll have to pay a stiff penalty — 10% plus taxes — on that "income." Falling behind on retirement account repayments can prove to be very expensive, indeed.

Another potential downside may surface if you leave your job. The entire loan may immediately become due. Most plans don't allow former employees to continue repaying in installments.

Finally, as Ted Benna of the 401(k) Association in Cross Fork, Pennsylvania warns, with a 401(k) loan you pay taxes twice. First, the interest and payments you make on the loan from your retirement fund will be made with after-tax dollars. Then, after you retire, you'll pay taxes on that same money when you withdraw it from your account.

## Example:

Let's say you borrow $10,000 from your 401(k) and pay it back at 9.5% interest over five years.

Monthly payment: $210
Total payments: $12,600  ($210 x 60 months)

To put aside $12,600, assuming you're in a 28% tax bracket,* you would have to earn $17,500 ($17,500 − $4,900 in taxes at 28% = $12,600).

Meanwhile, you'll be losing the interest you would have been earning on your 401(k) money, and then, come retirement time, you'll pay a second income tax upon withdrawal.

Also, when you borrow from your 401(k), you may have to pay an origination fee of $50 − $100, as well as an annual fee (generally around $50).

In the end, borrowing from your 401(k) may cost you far more than 9.5%.

## Success Strategies:

- **Borrow as little as possible. Repay it as quickly as you can.** That way, you can minimize the interest costs and fees you'll pay, as well as the time your money is out of your account, earning no return.

- **Don't borrow if your job is at all shaky.** Unless your plan allows you to continue to repay after you leave your job, you won't want to be both unemployed and trying to figure out how to immediately pay off that loan. It's a good idea to have a backup loan available (even if it's at a higher interest rate), such as a sufficient credit limit on a charge card, or a home equity line of credit, in case the worst does happen.

*Under the Economic Growth and Tax Relief Reconciliation Act of 2001, many of the tax rates will be reduced between 2001 and 2006.

- **Borrow, don't withdraw from your account.** If you *do* use retirement funds, be sure you borrow the money, rather than withdraw it. You'll pay a stiff penalty and immediate taxes on early withdrawals.

## Where to Shop:

Ask your plan administrator (who may be in the human resources or employee benefits department at work) for the details about loans under your plan. You may also need a financial professional to help you weigh the pros and cons of borrowing from your retirement account.

## Watch Out For:

**The temptation to borrow against your future.** Remember, the goal is to consolidate your debts, not compound your money troubles!

**Payment dates.** Pay close attention to the due dates, so you don't end up missing payments, and getting socked with penalties and taxes. See if you can have the funds automatically transferred from one of your accounts.

### Insurance Policy Loans

Your life insurance policy may also be an excellent place to go for an easy-to-get loan. With whole life, universal life, and variable life insurance, you can typically borrow up to 90% of its cash value. You can't borrow against term insurance because it has no "cash value."

## The Good News:

These loans are very easy to obtain, with no credit check required. Interest rates are often attractive, though sometimes misleading (see the next page). You can pay these loans back as quickly or as slowly as you like, or you can choose to not repay them at all.

## The Bad News:

Your loan reduces your death benefits, so if you pass away before the loan is repaid, there will be less insurance available to your family or other beneficiaries.

Although these loans are often touted as having "low" interest rates, the effective interest rate you'll pay is often higher than the stated rate. That's because the portion of the cash value you borrow against will earn a lower interest rate until the loan has been paid back.

For example, suppose your policy charges 8% on loans, and pays 7.5% on cash values — but reduces that interest rate to 5% on the amount of cash value that has been borrowed against. If you borrow $10,000 against your policy, the 7.5% your policy normally pays will drop to 5% on that $10,000 (a loss in interest of 2.5%). So, in effect, the loan is costing you not the 8% in interest the policy charges you, but that 8% plus the 2.5% loss in interest, which makes the effective interest rate 10.5%.

## Success Strategies:

- **Borrow only if your insurance needs have changed.** If your children have left the nest, or you have accumulated more assets, you may need less life insurance. If you don't require as much of a death benefit as you once did, a loan may make perfect sense. But if your insurance needs are unchanged or higher than they were (e.g., another baby) a loan may be devastating to your heirs if the worst should happen.

---

### What's the Value of Life Insurance Cash Value?

Let's say you've been paying and paying and paying the premiums on a life insurance policy that builds up a cash value.

If you've accumulated a cash value of, for example, $20,000 on a $100,000 policy, you might believe that you could withdraw your "savings" of $20,000 without costing your heirs the $100,000 death benefit.

Sorry. That's not how it works. If you borrow the $20,000 from a $100,000 policy, then travel up to those pearly gates, your beneficiary will receive $80,000, not $100,000.

---

- **Consider a term insurance policy.** If you have debt to pay down, discuss with your financial and insurance professionals whether a term policy would be more appropriate for your circumstances. If so, you can use the money you save to slash your debt.

## Where to Shop:

Ask your insurance company or agent for specific details about how a loan will affect your death benefits, cash value, and premium payments. Be sure to ask specifically about the interest rate you will have to pay, as well as the reduction in interest you will earn on the amount you borrow (the 2.5% in the example we just gave). Add them together to get the effective interest rate.

Some policies permit withdrawals of cash value, which can leave you without insurance. However, if your insurance needs have diminished, you might want to ask about a withdrawal.

## Watch Out For:

**Threats to the policy.** Before you withdraw money from your universal life policy, find out if you will still have enough cash value to keep the policy in force.

**Payments you hadn't planned on having to make.** If you are counting on your premiums being paid from the cash value, now or in the near future, a withdrawal could ruin that strategy, leaving you with higher out-of-pocket premium payments than you had planned.

**Interest-only payments that may be required.** If you don't make these payments, the interest will be subtracted from the cash value. Combined with any premium payments that come out of your cash value, you could end up with no cash to draw against, and a canceled policy.

**A tax bill.** You may incur taxable income by canceling your policy.

## How Much You Can Save:

If you borrow against your life insurance policy at an effective rate of 10.5% ...

> **If you have a $5,000 credit card balance at 17%**
> Pay it off in 3 years: You'll save $10,454
> Pay it off in 5 years: You'll save $9,856

> **If you have a $10,000 balance at 17%**
> Pay it off in 3 years: You'll save $21,746
> Pay it off in 5 years: You'll save $20,551

> **If you have a $15,000 balance at 17%**
> Pay it off in 3 years: You'll save $33,039
> Pay it off in 5 years: You'll save $31,246

## Margin or Savings Loans

If you have investments, you may have the ideal consolidation solution already at hand: cash in or borrow against your savings accounts, CDs, stocks, or bonds. (Note, we're not talking about money stashed in 401(k) or IRA accounts here; that's covered on pages 43 – 46.)

Loans against securities like mutual funds, stocks, or bonds are called "margin loans," and the interest rate on them has recently been in the 8.5% to 10% range, depending on the size of your portfolio and the amount you want to borrow.

Loans against passbook savings and other bank accounts fall into the category of "secured loans," and the interest rate on them usually ranges from 6% to 9%.

## The Good News:

Secured loans can be easier to qualify for than unsecured loans, because the lender can claim the collateral if the loan is not repaid. Since you are "securing" these loans with your savings, the rates are often more favorable, as well. But some of these loans may still require a credit check.

Margin loans do not require a credit check, but while you may be able to borrow up to 75% – 95% of the value of some bonds, you are usually limited to borrowing up to only 50% of the value of your stocks or mutual funds. Margin loan interest rates are usually attractive, and you don't have to make payments on these loans because you pay the interest when you sell the investments.

## The Bad News:

While saving money on your debts is important, depleting your rainy-day funds or borrowing against them to pay off your bills could prove nerve-racking, and maybe worse. If your investments are earning a paltry amount, and you know you can trust yourself not to get further into debt in the future, then feel free to tap into them. On the other hand, if your savings or investments are earning a reasonable rate of return and you don't feel as though you'll be able to replenish them any time soon, you might want to explore your other debt consolidation alternatives, and leave your nest egg alone.

*Note:* If the debt you are trying to pay down is high-interest credit card debt, it can prove smart to cash in your rainy-day savings. In an emergency, assuming you've stopped using those cards, you'd be able to charge airplane tickets to visit a sick parent, for example.

## Success Strategies:

- **Keep margin loans low.** If you keep margin borrowing at 20 – 25% of your investment account, you'll face little risk of a "margin call," unless the market really crashes. With a margin call, if the stock market value drops, you may be called on to immediately repay the loan, which may mean you'll need to sell stock at a time when the price you'll get will not be favorable.

- **Change your loan into savings.** If you have a hard time saving, you may want to borrow against your savings or securities, instead of wiping out your nest egg, even if the math is not as favorable as you'd like.

- **Set up a "bill" to pay yourself back.** If you do cash in your savings to pay off debts, consider asking your bank or credit union to deduct a fixed amount from your account each month toward a new savings or investment account. Start small, and you really won't miss it at all. Over time, gradually increase the amount you have transferred to your savings or investment account.

## Where to Shop:

Ask your banker, stock broker, or other investment professional for details on your options. For many people, the confusing question is whether to just withdraw the money from their account (or to cash in their investments), versus borrowing against the investment to pay off their debts.

To decide what would be in your best interest, first consider the interest or return you're earning. Subtract any fees, penalties (if you cash in a CD early, for example), or taxes you'd have to pay. For example, you'd pay capital gains taxes on profits when you sell stock. That will give you a net earnings figure. Then compare that figure with the interest you'd pay for borrowing against the investment. Based on the difference, you may be better off just taking the money out of the account and paying off your debts.

SLASH YOUR DEBT: Save Money and Secure Your Future

# Watch Out For:

**Margin loans against securities.** These can be especially dangerous. If the market declines and your investments drop in value, you'll face a "margin call" where you'll be required to put up more securities or money. If you can't come up with what you need, you'll have to sell some of your investments, which may trigger a tax bill and/or a loss. Avoid this strategy unless you have access to credit or other funds should your investments take a dive. And if you do have access to credit or other loan services, it may pay to investigate using them first.

**Unspecified terms/unspecified payments.** The other danger with margin loans is that there is no term — and no required payment. Be careful not to "tune out" this debt. Create your own repayment plan. Figure out how much you need to send in every month to pay off your margin loan in three to five years. (Table #5 on page 20 will make it easy.) Don't wait until you sell the stock to settle up. There might be nothing left!

## How Much You Can Save:

**If you get a margin loan at 10% ...**

| |
|---|
| **If you have a $5,000 credit card balance at 17%** <br> Pay it off in 3 years: You'll save $10,496 <br> Pay it off in 5 years: You'll save $9,930 |
| **If you have a $10,000 balance at 17%** <br> Pay it off in 3 years: You'll save $21,831 <br> Pay it off in 5 years: You'll save $20,699 |
| **If you have a $15,000 balance at 17%** <br> Pay it off in 3 years: You'll save $33,166 <br> Pay it off in 5 years: You'll save $31,468 |

"The game of life is not so much in holding
a good hand as playing a poor hand well."

– H. T. Leslie

# CHAPTER 5

# How to Improve Your Credit Rating ...

## to Get the Loans You Want

I f you're turned down for the consolidation loan you want, take consolation from the fact that you're in good company. Many lenders have rejection rates ranging from 60% to 75% or higher.

Of course, rejection is no fun. But it does give you an opportunity to get a new, perhaps more realistic perspective on your credit situation, especially if you treat it as a learning experience. (If you're desperate for a loan right now, you may not feel that way, but hang in there. The advice that follows may help.)

## What if They Say No?

- **Find out what the problem is.** By law, lenders must give you specific reasons why you were turned down. Make sure you receive and understand them. Answers like, "You do not meet our qualifications" don't suffice. On the other hand, don't expect answers that are extremely detailed. You might be told, for example, that you have too much debt in comparison to your income. But the lender may not say exactly how much is too much. If you do not get specific, understandable reasons for why you were turned down, ask for a better explanation.

- **Ask for advice.** Once you know the reasons you were turned down, ask the loan officer what you might be able to do so you *will* qualify for the loan, now or in the future. If you were turned down for a credit card, it may be harder to get a clear answer from the customer service department. Still, you might try talking with a supervisor to see if you can get any helpful advice.

- **Read the report.** If you were turned down due to information in your credit report, order a free copy immediately to find out what it says, and to make sure there are no mistakes. Your rejection letter will tell you how to request your free copy. This is perhaps *the* most important thing you can do if you have been turned down. Don't overlook this step. (Later, we'll show you how to improve your credit report.)

- **Go for it.** If it looks like you will be able to fix some of the rejection reasons in the next year or so, consider taking a slightly higher interest rate loan for now, and refinancing it later. Warning: This strategy can be risky because rates might go up. But they may also go down. In any event, taking whatever steps you can to cut your interest rate is always better than doing nothing.

- **Pare the plastic.** If you are turned down due to too much debt, ask if your application will be reconsidered if you close some accounts and cut up your cards. The lender might balk, knowing you could probably reactivate those cards easily, but it's certainly worth asking.

- **Did we say "shop"?** As we've said before, try at least three lenders. But don't apply for more than one loan at a time, since multiple applications (more than four or five in the last six months) can hurt your credit rating, especially when applying for credit cards.

SLASH YOUR DEBT: Save Money and Secure Your Future

- **Do it yourself.** Create your own "consolidation loan" by developing a plan for paying all your debts in a specific period of time, say five years. We'll show you how in Chapter 7.

- **Be patient.** Wait six months, pay as much as you can on your debts in the meantime, then reapply. Even if you don't get the new loan, if you send in just $25 a month more than the required amount every month on a $10,000 credit card bill at 17%, for example, you'll save $11,662 in interest and 33 years of payments (as shown in Table #9). This is not a typo … you'll save more than you borrowed!

| Table #9 | | | | | | | | | | | |
|---|---|---|---|---|---|---|---|---|---|---|---|
| **Dollars/Months Saved by Pre-Paying on Your Credit Card Bills** | | | | | | | | | | | |
| Card Balance | Monthly Pre-Payment | 11% | | 13% | | 15% | | 17% | | 19% | |
| | | Dollars | Mos | Dollars | Mos | Dollars | Mos | Dollars | Mos | Dollars | Mos |
| $1,500 | $ 3 | 245 | 45 | 379 | 55 | 600 | 73 | 1,003 | 102 | 1,856 | 159 |
| | $ 25 | 725 | 125 | 1,044 | 147 | 1,518 | 178 | 2,282 | 227 | 3,683 | 312 |
| | $ 50 | 843 | 143 | 1,193 | 166 | 1,704 | 198 | 2,510 | 249 | 3,960 | 335 |
| | $100 | 919 | 155 | 1,287 | 178 | 1,817 | 211 | 2,644 | 261 | 4,116 | 348 |
| $2,500 | $ 3 | 349 | 50 | 547 | 64 | 881 | 84 | 1,505 | 120 | 2,871 | 193 |
| | $ 25 | 1,178 | 150 | 1,725 | 180 | 2,559 | 221 | 3,937 | 287 | 6,530 | 405 |
| | $ 50 | 1,431 | 176 | 2,056 | 207 | 2,983 | 251 | 4,476 | 320 | 7,211 | 441 |
| | $100 | 1,611 | 193 | 2,282 | 225 | 3,261 | 270 | 4,813 | 339 | 7,616 | 462 |
| $3,500 | $ 3 | 421 | 53 | 663 | 67 | 1,078 | 90 | 1,862 | 129 | 3,610 | 209 |
| | $ 25 | 1,545 | 163 | 2,287 | 197 | 3,435 | 245 | 5,364 | 321 | 9,061 | 458 |
| | $ 50 | 1,942 | 194 | 2,815 | 230 | 4,129 | 282 | 6,270 | 363 | 10,246 | 505 |
| | $100 | 2,246 | 216 | 3,204 | 253 | 4,617 | 307 | 6,874 | 389 | 10,988 | 533 |
| $5,000 | $ 3 | 499 | 55 | 791 | 70 | 1,293 | 94 | 2,257 | 136 | 4,439 | 222 |
| | $ 25 | 1,991 | 175 | 2,979 | 212 | 4,533 | 266 | 7,192 | 352 | 12,396 | 509 |
| | $ 50 | 2,600 | 212 | 3,809 | 253 | 5,652 | 311 | 8,701 | 404 | 14,449 | 569 |
| | $100 | 3,111 | 239 | 4,475 | 282 | 6,506 | 342 | 9,786 | 438 | 15,821 | 606 |
| $7,500 | $ 3 | 589 | 56 | 939 | 72 | 1,546 | 97 | 2,723 | 141 | 5,429 | 232 |
| | $ 25 | 2,563 | 185 | 3,878 | 226 | 5,985 | 285 | 9,666 | 380 | 17,056 | 557 |
| | $ 50 | 3,498 | 228 | 5,185 | 273 | 7,802 | 339 | 12,211 | 444 | 20,693 | 633 |
| | $100 | 4,369 | 261 | 6,348 | 310 | 9,337 | 379 | 14,227 | 489 | 23,347 | 684 |
| $10,000 | $ 3 | 655 | 58 | 1,045 | 73 | 1,729 | 99 | 3,060 | 144 | 6,153 | 237 |
| | $ 25 | 3,004 | 191 | 4,580 | 233 | 7,134 | 295 | *11,662* | *397* | 20,921 | 585 |
| | $ 50 | 4,227 | 237 | 6,317 | 285 | 9,601 | 356 | 15,211 | 468 | 26,181 | 673 |
| | $100 | 5,451 | 275 | 7,982 | 327 | 11,846 | 402 | 18,237 | 521 | 30,297 | 734 |

*Table #9 is continued on page 56*

## Table #9 (continued)

# Dollars/Months Saved by Pre-Paying on Your Credit Card Bills

| Card Balance | Monthly Pre-Payment | 11% Dollars | Mos | 13% Dollars | Mos | 15% Dollars | Mos | 17% Dollars | Mos | 19% Dollars | Mos |
|---|---|---|---|---|---|---|---|---|---|---|---|
| $12,500 | $ 3 | 705 | 58 | 1,129 | 74 | 1,872 | 100 | 3,326 | 145 | 6,729 | 240 |
| | $ 25 | 3,363 | 194 | 5,156 | 237 | 8,086 | 302 | 13,336 | 407 | 24,226 | 604 |
| | $ 50 | 4,840 | 243 | 7,279 | 293 | 11,148 | 367 | 17,832 | 485 | 31,081 | 700 |
| | $ 100 | 6,400 | 284 | 9,432 | 339 | 14,099 | 419 | 21,895 | 544 | 36,756 | 770 |
| $15,000 | $ 3 | 747 | 58 | 1,198 | 74 | 1,990 | 101 | 3,545 | 146 | 7,200 | 243 |
| | $ 25 | 3,666 | 197 | 5,643 | 241 | 8,897 | 307 | 14,777 | 414 | 27,109 | 617 |
| | $ 50 | 5,370 | 247 | 8,116 | 299 | 12,505 | 375 | 20,159 | 496 | 35,501 | 721 |
| | $ 100 | 7,246 | 291 | 10,734 | 348 | 16,144 | 431 | 25,256 | 561 | 42,784 | 798 |
| $20,000 | $ 3 | 813 | 58 | 1,307 | 75 | 2,177 | 101 | 3,892 | 149 | 7,954 | 245 |
| | $ 25 | 4,159 | 200 | 6,441 | 245 | 10,232 | 313 | 17,169 | 425 | 31,968 | 635 |
| | $ 50 | 6,252 | 253 | 9,519 | 306 | 14,804 | 385 | 24,152 | 513 | 43,233 | 749 |
| | $ 100 | 8,703 | 300 | 12,999 | 360 | 19,742 | 447 | 31,258 | 587 | 53,763 | 839 |
| $25,000 | $ 3 | 864 | 59 | 1,391 | 76 | 2,322 | 102 | 4,164 | 149 | 8,545 | 247 |
| | $ 25 | 4,551 | 202 | 7,078 | 248 | 11,306 | 317 | 19,112 | 431 | 35,970 | 646 |
| | $ 50 | 6,970 | 257 | 10,670 | 312 | 16,705 | 392 | 27,499 | 524 | 49,839 | 768 |
| | $ 100 | 9,930 | 306 | 14,923 | 368 | 22,836 | 458 | 36,499 | 603 | 63,558 | 866 |
| $30,000 | $ 3 | 906 | 60 | 1,460 | 75 | 2,442 | 102 | 4,388 | 150 | 9,030 | 248 |
| | $ 25 | 4,878 | 204 | 7,610 | 249 | 12,206 | 319 | 20,748 | 435 | 39,373 | 654 |
| | $ 50 | 7,576 | 259 | 11,645 | 314 | 18,328 | 397 | 30,381 | 531 | 55,608 | 781 |
| | $ 100 | 10,989 | 311 | 16,596 | 373 | 25,551 | 466 | 41,155 | 615 | 72,402 | 886 |
| $40,000 | $ 3 | 973 | 59 | 1,570 | 76 | 2,631 | 103 | 4,740 | 150 | 9,799 | 250 |
| | $ 25 | 5,402 | 205 | 8,465 | 252 | 13,658 | 324 | 23,404 | 440 | 44,950 | 665 |
| | $ 50 | 8,562 | 262 | 13,239 | 319 | 20,998 | 404 | 35,165 | 541 | 65,326 | 799 |
| | $ 100 | 12,753 | 316 | 19,402 | 381 | 30,148 | 478 | 49,140 | 631 | 87,864 | 915 |
| $50,000 | $ 3 | 1,024 | 59 | 1,655 | 76 | 2,777 | 103 | 5,015 | 151 | 10,399 | 250 |
| | $ 25 | 5,813 | 206 | 9,140 | 254 | 14,808 | 325 | 25,517 | 443 | 49,426 | 670 |
| | $ 50 | 9,347 | 263 | 14,515 | 321 | 23,147 | 407 | 39,051 | 547 | 73,330 | 810 |
| | $ 100 | 14,189 | 319 | 21,704 | 386 | 33,952 | 484 | 55,834 | 641 | 101,077 | 933 |

Note: These amounts were calculated with The Banker's Secret Credit Card Software, and are based on minimum required payments that are 2% of the monthly balance, with a $10 minimum.

## Credit Reports

You can think of your credit report as a report card describing how you've handled your bills in the past. It lists your credit accounts and whether you have paid them on time. There are three major companies that compile credit reports: Equifax, Experian (formerly TRW), and Trans Union. These companies collect information from lenders about how you pay your bills, and then compile that information into credit reports, which are sold to lenders, insurance companies, car dealers, and even to landlords and employers.

Your credit report is the key to getting the consolidation loans you want. It's so important, because lenders rely on information about how you've handled your bills in the past to decide if you're likely to pay this new one on time. If your credit report is less than perfect, don't despair. In a few pages, we'll show you how to improve it. In the meantime, it may be helpful to understand how credit reports work.

There are four basic types of information on credit reports. The first is personal identifying information: your name, current and previous addresses, Social Security number, birth date, and (if you have one) your spouse's name. You may also find information about where you've worked, but it's not uncommon for that information to be omitted or out of date on credit reports.

Credit information makes up the second — and most important part — of your credit report. This section contains details about your credit cards and other loans, including when you opened those accounts, your highest balance, your current balance, and your payment history. Your payment history goes back indefinitely for positive information, but only about seven years for negative information such as late payments, and up to 10 years for bankruptcies.

The third part of your credit report is public record information, if there is any. This can include any tax liens, court judgments against you, or overdue child support. Again, negative information like this can stay on your credit report for some seven years.

Finally, your credit report will contain a list of inquiries, showing who has accessed your credit report in the past couple of years. It will probably include companies that have reviewed your report for "pre-approved" credit offers. Inquiries related to pre-approved offers will show up on your credit report when you request a copy, but *will not* be given to lenders who request a copy. So those inquiries won't be counted against you when you apply for credit.

**O━🗝 KEY POINT** *The key to building and keeping a great credit report is to avoid late payments, and to have at least one major credit card that you pay on time, and over time.* It's the single strongest reference on a credit report. The reason? Statistics have shown that people who have paid major credit cards on time in the past are likely to pay new ones on time, too.

## How to Get Your Credit Report:

When you're turned down for a loan or credit card based on information in your credit file, you can get a copy of your credit report for free. Contact the bureau listed on the denial letter within 60 days to request one. (You can also get a free copy of your report if you are unemployed and looking for work, or are on public assistance.)

If you fear a serious mistake on your report, or if you haven't been turned down for a loan but want to check your report anyway (which is a great idea!), you can order a copy of your report from any of the following agencies:

**Equifax:**
800-685-1111 or
www.equifax.com

**Experian:**
888-EXPERIAN (888-397-3742)
www.experian.com

**Trans Union:**
800-888-4213
www.transunion.com

The cost is typically $8, except in the following states, where you can generally get one for free: Colorado, Georgia, Maryland, Massachusetts, New Jersey, and Vermont. In case you're wondering, it really doesn't matter which bureau you get a copy from, since all three operate nationwide and are likely to have similar information.

When you get your credit report, look for outdated or incorrect information. If you find any, use the form enclosed with your report to tell the credit bureau of the mistake. Include copies of any documentation that back up your version of the story. (Keep the originals, along with a copy of the form.) The credit bureau and lender are required to consider what you send in during their investigation.

Make sure what you write on the form is clear, to the point, and understandable. (You may be tempted to blast the bureau for having wrong information, but it's not the wisest approach. Stick to the facts as you know them.) You might want to ask a friend or relative to review your form before you send it.

The credit bureau has 30 days, by law, to investigate and get back to you with its results. What the bureau will do is go to the lender with your dispute. If the lender's files show something different, and they stick with their version, the bureau will probably write to tell you the information has been verified and will stay on your report. In that case, you're going to have to contact the lender directly and try to straighten it out with someone who works there. Once you've had the dispute resolved, ask for a correction to be sent in to the credit bureau.

You do have leverage: The Consumer Credit Reporting Reform Act of 1996 forbids lenders from reporting information they "know or consciously avoid knowing" is wrong.

Keep in mind that what you think is a mistake may not be. Here are some little-known facts about credit reports:

- **Your report lists accounts that you have paid off.** Even if you have paid an account in full, it can remain on your credit report. Negative information like collection accounts, late payments, or defaults, can stay on your credit report for up to about seven years, even if you ultimately paid the bill in full.

- **Your report lists information about bills you shared with your ex-spouse.** Joint accounts you shared with your ex can be listed on your report for about seven years (if the information is negative) or indefinitely (if it's positive). That applies even if your ex was assigned those bills during the divorce. But accounts you never shared with him or her should not be on your report.

- **Your report contains information you've been arguing about with a lender.** Credit bureaus aren't required to make judgments about who's right and who's wrong in disputes. Unless they have evidence that a creditor is reporting wrong information, they will likely take the lender's word in disputes.

- **Your report is missing some accounts.** Nothing requires a lender to report information to a credit bureau, and not all do. You can ask to have unlisted accounts added to your report, but it probably won't do much good as far as building credit is concerned, since they won't be updated very often, if at all.

If you can't get information you believe is wrong taken off your report, you can ask the bureau to add a 100-word statement explaining your side of the story. Whether or not that will help depends on the situation. If your application is reviewed by a computer, which many are, it's probably not going to help. But if your application is reviewed by a loan officer, the statement can help back up what you've hopefully discussed already.

For further help in straightening out errors on your credit report, we recommend the *Do-It-Yourself Credit Repair Guide*, by Paul Richard.*

## What Does It Say?

Some credit reports are easier to read than others. Although they've improved a lot over the past decade, don't be surprised if you find something on yours that you don't understand. If there is anything on your report that you don't understand, call the credit bureau and ask for an explanation. (They're required to give you one.) Make sure it's all clear to you.

## What Does It Mean?

That's a whole 'nother story! Even lenders, seeing the facts in black and white, don't always know what's "good" and what's "bad." These days, they usually rely on "credit scoring" systems to help them decide who gets a loan and who doesn't.

---

*This and all books recommended in *Slash Your Debt* are available from:
Good Advice Press, P.O. Box 78, Elizaville, NY 12523, 914-758-1400.
Or visit our Web site: www.goodadvicepress.com.

## Credit Scoring: Getting Card or Loan Approval

When it comes to credit cards, the decision about whether or not to give you credit is usually all in the numbers. Here's how it works:

Typically, when you apply for a credit card, your application goes to a processing center, where a data-entry clerk enters your personal information into a computer. As long as you meet the basic requirements (you make their required minimum income, for example), the computer dials up a credit bureau and gets your credit report information. Then, without human review, you'll be evaluated by that bank's unpublicized, ever-changing credit scoring system ... a statistical profile used by that lender's own "R2D2" to decide how much of a risk you are. If you get a passing score, you'll get the card. If not, you'll probably receive a computer-generated rejection letter. Although at some banks, if you fall into a "gray area" between those people who are automatically approved and those who are rejected, your information may be sent to a loan officer for a final decision.

How do the computers know which applications to accept? They're programmed using *credit scoring systems*. With a scoring system, the goal is to compare the things people who pay their bills on time have in common with each other, and what things people who don't pay their bills have in common, and then to use those factors to predict whether a potential new customer is likely to always pay on time.

Some of the factors that may be included in a scoring system are how many credit cards you have, what other types of loans you have, how many times you've been late on payments, how much you owe on all your bills, etc.

Once the lender has analyzed its accounts to determine which factors are most likely to predict whether bills will be paid on time, those factors go into its scoring system, with points assigned to each one. Each lender has a different system for determining whether they think an applicant will be a good risk. Unfortunately, lenders don't divulge all the details of the factors they consider, or the weight they give to each factor. And there are many different types of scoring systems, and some lenders use more than one type of score for each application.

**KEY POINT** *What's most important to understand about scoring is that there are no quick fixes. You can't change your credit* *score overnight to "fit the profile" of people who pay their bills on time.*

Although each creditor may use its own scoring system, many will look at the answers you give to some or all of the following questions. So whether you want to consolidate debt onto a low-rate card, or to rebuild credit following a bankruptcy or other financial problem, consider how you would answer the following questions:

## 1. Do you pay your bills on time?

Almost all lenders will look at whether you've been late paying your other bills. Though some lenders want to see absolutely no late payments, most are a little more lenient, and won't score against you for a 30-day late payment or two (but not 60 or 90 days), provided they happened more than a year ago.

While some may actually tolerate a lot of late payments, most lenders won't take you if you're currently behind on your accounts, so catch up before you apply.

## 2. Have you had any serious money troubles?

A car repossessed? Accounts that were sent to collections? Your home foreclosed? A judgment or tax lien issued against you? If so, it's not going to be easy to get credit. Make sure your slate is as clean as you can get it. If you've paid the judgment, for example, verify that it's marked "paid" on your credit report. See our strategies for rebuilding credit, starting on page 68.

## 3. Have you declared bankruptcy?

While some banks will turn you down for this in a heartbeat, don't assume that you'll automatically be disqualified. There are some lenders who will take you on, especially if the bankruptcy is several years in the past, and you've since established other credit references that you've paid on time.

## 4. How close are you to your credit limits?

Lenders compare your credit card balances to the total amount of credit you have available. Usually, if you have a lot of credit cards and are very close to your limits on them, you'll not score as well with the electronic evaluators. We'll say it again: Pay down that revolving debt!

## 5. How many of your recently opened accounts have balances?

Try not to carry much of a balance on accounts you've opened in the past six months to a year, including any balances you might have transferred. Two or more new cards with balances can be a red flag.

## 6. How many credit cards do you have?

A currently held Visa, MasterCard, Discover, or American Express card, which you've paid on time, over time, can be your strongest credit reference if you're applying for a credit card. It's usually better than a mortgage or a car loan. Why? Because mortgages and car loans are "secured," backed by the house or vehicle, whereas credit cards are unsecured. And since banks like to play "follow the leader," if one lender has trusted you to borrow money based on your signature alone, others are sure to follow.

But don't go overboard. While a couple of major credit cards are usually enough to demonstrate a good credit rating, you don't want too many of them. If you already have six or seven bankcards, don't call and cancel a bunch of them at once. That can hurt your score. If you're transferring a balance from one card to another, that's a good time to close an account.

## 7. How many "tradelines" are there on your credit report?

In plain English, this means how many mortgages, credit cards, student loans, and personal loans do you have? Having several tradelines — but not too many — will improve your score. It's impossible to say what "too many tradelines" will be, since every scoring system is different. The longer your credit history, the more tradelines you'll be expected to have.

## 8. What's your "debt-to-income ratio" excluding your mortgage?

Although this ratio isn't used much in credit card lending, it is used in scoring for mortgages and car loans. Here's an example: If a quarter of your salary goes toward payments on your credit cards and car loan, then your "debt-to-income ratio" would be 25%. When it comes to the percent of your monthly pay that is taken up by debt payments, less is better. You'll never be considered a bad credit risk because you don't carry much debt … as long as you do have credit.

## 9. How many inquiries are there on your credit report?

Every time a lender orders a copy of your credit report, an "inquiry" is placed on your credit file. Lenders get nervous if lots of others have requested copies of your credit report. Although inquiries for the last two years will show, most scoring systems are particularly concerned with recent inquiries — those within the past year.

While an inquiry doesn't indicate whether you got the loan, statistics show that people who have recently applied for a lot of credit are less likely to pay their bills on time. So if you have four or more inquiries on your report in the past six months, wait a few months before applying for another loan or card.

Fair, Isaac, a company that develops most credit scoring systems, says that it has several programs in place to protect consumers shopping for auto and home loans. Under its system, any inquiries within a seven-day period are treated as a single inquiry. In addition, all auto and mortgage-related inquiries in the 30 days before the score is compiled are ignored. Auto and home loan inquiries older than 30 days, but that occur within a 14-day stretch, are treated as a single inquiry. Fair, Isaac also says that in its credit scoring system, inquiries have only a slight effect on the credit score.

*Note:* You may notice some inquiries on your credit report marked "consumer" or "promotional." A consumer inquiry means you got your own report, and a promotional inquiry means your file was reviewed for a pre-approved credit card. Neither appears on reports sent to lenders.

## 10. How old are you?

This factor isn't used very often. When it is, it's against the law to discriminate against someone 62 or older. For example, a lender may find that people in their thirties have a lot of debts, or people in their twenties haven't learned how to manage credit very well … and score you accordingly.

## What's Your Final Score?

The better you score, the greater your chances will be of getting the debt consolidation loan you want, putting that new card in your wallet, financing that new addition to your castle, you name it! Pay your bills on time, don't charge more than you can afford, and you'll be all set!

## How Long Can Information Stay on Your Credit Report?

Negative information, like late payments or collection accounts, can generally be kept on your report for no more than seven years and six months from the date the payments should have been made. So if the payment was due December 1, 1998, it can stay on your report until June 1, 2006.

Credit laws, like most legalese, are at best impenetrable, so stay with us a minute. Under the old credit reporting law (before 1996), there were some exceptions to this time frame, which made things rather confusing — to say the least. So Congress amended the law to make the reporting period for negative information clearer. But the new rules only cover information added to a credit report on or after January 1, 1998.

The new law says that any negative information (except bankruptcy) added to a credit report on or after January 1, 1998 can be reported for no more than seven years and six months from the date the original payment was due. Even if an account is later turned over to a collection agency, that seven years and six months reporting period applies.

Bankruptcies can legally be reported for 10 years from the date you filed. But the major credit bureaus have agreed voluntarily to remove Chapter 13 bankruptcies (where you pay back some or all of your debts over several years) after seven years from the date of filing.

## The Good Old Days

If there is information on your credit report that was reported earlier than January 1, 1998, then the old law and the following rules apply:

**Judgments:** A court judgment is a piece of paper ordering you to pay someone who has sued you and won. Unpaid judgments can be logged for up to 20 years, depending on the laws in your state. Paid judgments will appear for seven years from the date a judgment was entered by the court.

**Tax liens:** Unpaid tax liens may remain indefinitely until they are paid. Paid tax liens can show for as many as seven years from the date they were paid.

**Collection accounts:** They'll haunt you for seven years from the date they were turned over to a collection agency.

**Charged-off accounts:** A charge-off is an account the lender wrote off as a bad debt because it wasn't paid. It will be listed as a "charge-off," "profit-and-loss," or an "R-09" on your credit report. And there it will stay for seven years from the date it was charged off.

**Positive information:** No time limit.

## Check Verification — One More Credit Woe

There's a whole other tier of credit bureaus that are just becoming known to consumers: check verification services. Often when you're paying by check in, for example, a department store, you'll see the clerk clear your check by phone or through a computer terminal. He or she is probably dialing a check verification bureau that generally gives the green light to your payment if you don't have a record of bounced checks.

If, however, you've bounced a check with some other merchant, it's quite possible you got reported to one of the check verification companies. If you come up with a "record," and you've never bounced a check, you might well be the victim of forgery. And you could also get rejected if your perfectly good check is deemed "high risk," as explained by executives at Equifax, one of the check verification bureaus.

For example, if a Miami computer store has decided that large checks presented in the evening stand a good chance of being forgeries, the check will be flagged. If Equifax's computers can't find a "positive record" on you, information that you satisfy their criteria for a good check-writing history, or other information that confirms your check is likely to be "good," your check may be rejected. In that case, Equifax would help you set up a positive record to avoid being rejected again.

You would fill out a form with bank information that's verified with your bank to establish you as a good customer.

Whether or not you think the information is accurate, you have the right to find out what's on file under your name. In fact, the merchant who refused your check must provide you with information on how to get the report used to reject your payment.

Unlike credit bureaus that maintain your credit record — good and bad — on one file, these check verification services may have separate sets of files: a negative file if there's been negative information reported by a merchant and a positive one if you have a good track record. According to the U.S. Public Interest Research Group (U.S. PIRG), having a negative record with one of these outfits could stand in the way of getting a loan or even opening a checking account, so it's important to clear up any inaccuracies in your files.

While credit bureaus generally will not give specific information on your file over the phone, the check verification companies may tell you the details of your negative file when you call. You'll need to provide your driver's license number and the account numbers on the bottom of one of your checks, along with other personal information to identify you, such as your date of birth. (The merchant that rejected your check should provide you with the name of the check verification service it used.) To check on the information or to report suspected fraudulent activity, Paul Richard of the National Center for Financial Education (www.ncfe.org) recommends contacting the following companies:

| | |
|---|---|
| **ChexSystems** | 800-428-9623 |
| **CheckRite** | 800-766-2748 |
| **SCAN** | 800-262-7771 |
| **TeleCheck** | 800-710-9898 (forgery reports) |
| | 800-927-0188 (inquiries on bounced checks) |
| **Equifax** | 800-437-5120 |
| **NPC** | 800-526-5380 |

There are also separate bureaus that collect information on apartment evictions. And U.S. PIRG reports that telephone companies are setting up a clearinghouse to report and share information.

Even though thousands of issuers are heavily competing for a spot in most people's wallet, getting that first card, or trying to re-establish credit after serious money troubles, can seem like an impossible task.

Even if you have a good job, a mortgage, and a car loan, it's possible you could still be turned down for a bank card because of an "insufficient credit history." If you've never had a credit card before, lenders have no way of knowing how responsible you'll be should times get tough. They reason that most people would pay their mortgages and car loans first, letting credit card bills slide. The last thing card issuers want to do is take a chance. Hence, a good old-fashioned Catch 22: How do you get credit experience if no one will give you that first card?

Or perhaps your credit applications keep being denied because you had some hard times a while ago, although you eventually paid the bills. How can you get credit again?

Discouraged? Don't be.

**KEY POINT** *The key to re-establishing credit is to build new positive credit references.* Eventually, the bad information becomes less important to lenders who will see that you're now on top of your finances. Here's what to do:

**Check your credit report.** We told you how to get a copy on page 58. You won't know what lenders know about your credit history unless you get a copy, so do it — even if you'd rather not know what's on there. Make sure everything is correct and up-to-date on your report. If any accounts listed on your credit report show that you're currently behind on payments, get caught up before you apply for credit.

**Get a secured card.** Secured MasterCard and Visa cards can be a great way to establish and re-establish credit. You open a savings account with the bank that offers the card, and you get a major credit card that you can use just like any other Visa or MasterCard. Your credit limit is generally 100% to 150% of the amount of security you've deposited with the bank. No one will know it's secured except you and the bank.

From our point of view, being limited to charge only what you can afford is an obvious advantage — you won't get in over your head.

There's another secured card advantage that's often overlooked: You'll probably earn more interest on the security deposit than you would at a local bank.

On the downside, secured cards usually come with a high interest rate, which won't affect you in the slightest if you only charge what you can really afford, then pay the bill off every month.

When you can't pay in full, pay as much over the required minimum as you can. By always paying more than the minimum, you'll save a fortune in interest. In any case, you must send in a payment. It will not be taken from your security deposit. And never be late with a payment, even if all you're sending in is the minimum.

Although they're usually much easier to get than the more typical unsecured credit cards (cards that don't require a savings deposit), most secured cards are not "guaranteed." You'll have to earn enough to meet the bank's minimum income requirement, and you may not qualify if you're behind on bills when you apply, or have unpaid tax liens or court judgments against you. Some issuers will give cards to people with very recent bankruptcies; others want you to wait a year after your bankruptcy is finished before you apply. Check with the issuing bank if you're not sure you'll qualify.

**Important:** To make sure your secured card will help establish or bolster your credit rating, confirm that the issuing bank reports to the three major credit bureaus. If not, all your hard work and good payment habits will be in vain.

*Even more important:* Make sure you're applying for a legitimate MasterCard or Visa. There are plenty of scam deals out there, and you don't want to be ripped off. You can get a list of genuine secured cards from any of the following sources:

**Myvesta (formerly Debt Counselors of America)** ($5 by mail). Myvesta Secured Card List, P.O. Box 8587, Gaithersburg, MD 20898-8587, or visit www.myvesta.org. This list is updated several times a year.

**CardTrak** ($5). CardTrak Secured List, P.O. Box 1700, Frederick, MD 21702, or visit www.cardtrak.com. This list is updated monthly.

# Credit Repair

If you've had credit problems in the past, you may be tempted to sign on with an outfit that promises to erase your bad credit history. Don't! There are no special legal loopholes they can use to clean up your credit.

For a good healthy fee, these scam artists will keep disputing negative information that's on your credit report, even though it may be accurate. Their hope is that some of it won't be verified and will therefore have to be removed.

Unfortunately, once the credit bureaus suspect that a "credit repair clinic" is involved, they can refuse to even investigate the disputed information. In the end, your wallet will be lighter, but your bad credit rating will be intact.

Here are some of the important restrictions that were created in the Credit Repair Organizations Act of 1996:

- Credit clinics can't make any statement that is untrue or misleading, or tell a consumer to do that either. So it's against the law for them to tell you to give the credit bureau inaccurate information.

- Credit clinics can't accept payment until they've already performed the services they promise. Don't pay upfront!

- You must get a signed, dated contract that explains the services that will be performed and when they'll be performed, any guarantees offered, and the cost. You have three business days to cancel the contract without penalty.

## Yet More Routes to Credit

**Get a co-signer and take out a loan.** It's best to go this route when you don't really need to borrow money. It can work one of two ways: You can be the primary borrower (you take out the loan and the other person co-signs), or the other person can be the primary borrower and you can co-sign. As long as the payments are made on time, you'll improve your credit either way. (Don't forget to make sure the bank reports payments to all three bureaus before you apply.)

Put the money you borrow in a savings account so you don't have to worry about whether you'll be able to make the payments, then pay the loan back early. The fact that you paid the loan off will improve your credit.

We've said it before: Don't risk a friendship or relationship over a loan! If you are late on any payments, it will go on both credit reports — yours and your co-borrower's — and will look just as bad on both. And both of you will be legally responsible to the lender if payments aren't made. Ask someone to help you out only if you are absolutely, 150% certain you can make every payment on time.

**Take advantage of someone else's good credit.** This is similar to the previous step, but you won't have to borrow any money yourself. Ask a relative or good friend to add you to their major credit card account as a co-signer or joint applicant. They'll have to call their card issuer for instructions, but usually you will have to sign an application to be added. Once you are on the account, it will be listed on your credit report as a joint account and can be an excellent credit reference — provided the bills are paid on time.

Make sure you are added onto the account as a *co-signer* or *joint applicant,* not just as an authorized user, which won't help much as a credit reference. Keep in mind you'll be responsible for the bills if the other person can't or won't pay, and their credit report will be blemished if you're expected to make the payments, but you don't.

**Create a spending plan** so you'll be able to manage your money better, and won't have to rely so much on credit. (See Chapter 9.) If you feel like you'll never get ahead, you may want to make an appointment with a debt counselor to review your spending habits and suggest changes. See Chapter 6 for more information.

## Q & A

**Q:** **The attorney who handled my bankruptcy assured me that after I completed it, I would have no trouble getting credit because I would no longer have any debts. Why do I keep getting rejected?**

**A:** Most people who file for bankruptcy find it hard to get credit afterward, no matter what their attorney may say. When they do get credit — a mortgage, for example — they usually have to come up with larger down payments and pay much higher interest rates or fees. Bankruptcy doesn't just "wipe the slate clean" for a couple of reasons.

First, each of the accounts that you filed in your bankruptcy — the credit cards or other loans — can now be listed on your credit report for up to seven years and six months as "charge-offs" or "filed in bankruptcy," both of which are negative marks on a credit report.

Secondly, the fact that you filed for bankruptcy can stay on your credit report for seven to 10 years from the date of filing, depending on what type of bankruptcy you filed. (Ten years for a Chapter 7 "straight" bankruptcy, where you get rid of some or all of your debts right away, or seven years for a Chapter 13 "wage earner's" bankruptcy, where you pay back some or all of your debts over several years.)

It's not impossible to get credit after bankruptcy, but it does take more work to rebuild your credit and prove to lenders that you have good control over your finances. See "No Credit? Bad Credit? You CAN Get a Card" on page 68 for more post-bankruptcy advice.

**Q: I got behind a few months on one bill when I was between jobs, but as soon as I could, I made a large payment to make up for it. Doesn't that help?**

**A:** Yes and no. The problem is that your credit report won't show that you made a larger payment one month. It only shows whether or not you made the required monthly payments on time each month. Of course, the sooner you pay down a bill, the less money you owe, and the fact that you have less debt can help your credit. Still, don't let yourself fall into this trap. Get at least those minimum payments in the mail on time, all the time.

**Q: I had perfect credit for many years before I ran into financial problems. Now I feel like all the credit card companies do is look at the recent bad information, but they won't take into account the fact that I paid my bills on time for so long. It seems completely unfair!**

**A:** As we explained before in the section about credit scoring, lenders are interested in what kind of risk you are — statistically speaking. Recent information usually carries more weight than older information. So unfortunately, you're going to have to rebuild your credit as we've described.

However, if you have a long-term relationship with a bank or credit union, you may be able to get more favorable treatment in person, by sitting down with a lender to explain what happened and why you're on better financial footing now. Sometimes, it helps to remind a lender that there are other places where you could just as easily move your accounts.

**Q: I obtained a secured credit card to rebuild my credit. A friend told me I will build my credit faster if I charge a big purchase and pay it off over several months, but I am not thrilled about the high finance charge. What should I do?**

**A:** Do it your way! As far as your credit report goes, you can charge a large purchase and pay it off over time, or charge a smaller purchase and pay it off right away. Credit reports don't show how much you paid, they just show whether or not you make at least the minimum required payment each month. But if you run up large bills and don't pay them off right away, it could look like you have a lot of debt, and you may spend a lot on finance charges — neither of which is a benefit. So listen to us, not your friend! You're on the right track.

When you do get a major credit card, secured or unsecured, use it on a regular basis for purchases you'd make anyway, then pay the bills in full as soon as you can. That way you'll keep the account active, but won't risk getting in over your head or paying any more in interest than absolutely necessary.

**Q: Does paying rent and utility bills on time help rebuild my credit?**

**A:** Probably not. Rent, utility bills, medical bills, most gasoline credit cards, and some smaller retail accounts usually are not reported to credit bureaus, unless you are late with your payments. The credit bureaus are looking into the feasibility of including some of this information, though, and may include it in the future. Remember, no company is required to report information to credit bureaus, and some don't bother.

*"More and more these days I find myself pondering on how to reconcile my net income with my gross habits."*

– John Kirk Nelson

# Getting Help — Credit and Debt Counseling

I f you aren't able to obtain a debt consolidation loan — perhaps because you already have too much debt or your credit history isn't great — a nonprofit credit or debt counseling service may be able to help. Although they don't actually consolidate debts, they can set up a payment plan in which you make one monthly payment to the counseling agency, which then pays each of your creditors.

These organizations can also save you money by negotiating lower payments and/or lower interest rates with your creditors. Some also offer budget counseling, usually at minimal cost to the client.

## Some of the Nonprofit Organizations Offering These Services Include:

**Myvesta**
800-680-3328
www.myvesta.org

Myvesta (formerly Debt Counselors of America) is the nation's first nonprofit Internet-based debt counseling agency. Visit its Web site, which offers many free and low-cost educational tools, as well as traditional repayment programs, for those trying to reduce their debt. Myvesta's staff includes attorneys and certified financial planners (CFPs). Gerri Detweiler, one of the authors of this book, is education advisor for Myvesta.

**National Foundation for Consumer Credit**
800-388-2227
www.nfcc.org

This is the umbrella organization for thousands of different credit counseling agencies across the country. Each operates independently, so choose carefully. We'll explain how you can do that, below.

## The Good News:

Because of their contacts with the credit industry, these organizations are generally able to negotiate better repayment terms with creditors than you could do on your own. Similar to a consolidation loan, once you are following a repayment plan, you'll only make one monthly payment to the counseling service. Most people can get out of debt in three to five years on one of these plans (not including secured debts such as a mortgage).

Some counseling services will even debit your monthly payment directly from your bank account. The fees for credit counseling are minimal, or even free to the consumer, because the agencies are paid by lenders.

## The Bad News:

Even if your creditors agree to a lower payment and/or interest rate under one of these programs, a few may report to the credit bureaus that your account is being repaid through credit counseling, or that you are late, since technically, you are not making your originally agreed-upon payments. However, the very large majority of lenders will actually bring your account current, and report it as current as long as you follow through with the counseling program. Ask the counselor for specific information about how each of your individual accounts will be reported to the credit bureaus.

The services that counseling agencies provide vary widely, and some are much better than others. So choose carefully. You want a counseling agency that will help you successfully conquer your bills — not get you deeper into debt. (It happens!) Don't work with a counseling agency if you feel pressured or uncomfortable.

With an explosion in the number of credit and debt counseling agencies today, it's not surprising that consumers are sometimes confused about their options. It can be difficult to distinguish between organizations providing a high level of service and education, and those that operate more like collection agencies for creditors, by pushing consumers into repayment plans.

To help consumers evaluate their options, Myvesta (formerly Debt Counselors of America) has given us permission to reprint the following questions. You may want to ask them of a prospective counseling agency. We've added the explanations that follow each question.

## Questions to Ask a Credit or Debt Counseling Agency

1. *Can I get information on your agency and programs?* Don't be pressured by an agency that insists on signing you up on the spot, over the phone.

2. *Do you pay referral fees to others who refer consumers for counseling?* If the agency pays finders' fees for new business, it may be more interested in getting people on payment plans than in providing assistance or education.

3. *What should I do if I cannot afford the minimum payment?* Ideally, an agency should offer a hardship program, rather than telling you your only option is bankruptcy.

4. *What kind of training do you have that makes you qualified to assist me?* Although it's hard to judge credentials, some counselors are really nothing more than telemarketers who are paid to sign up as many people as possible for repayment programs.

5. *What security measures do you take to protect my information?* Your personal and account information is extremely confidential and should be carefully protected against unauthorized access.

6. *Can I get up-to-date, regular reports on the status of my accounts?* You need to be able to tell if the counseling agency is, in fact, paying all your creditors on time. Find out how you will be able to monitor your account.

7. *Can you answer my general questions, even if I am not in your repayment program?* A counseling agency should provide a basic level of assistance, even to people who are not enrolled in a payment program.

8. *What kinds of educational programs and services do you provide?* Educational programs are important to help you solve your financial problems and learn positive new habits. You can tell a lot about an agency by the quality of its educational materials and services.

9. *Is there a minimum amount of debt I have to have in order to work with you?* Some agencies will turn you away if you don't have "enough" debt. But what may not seem like a lot to someone at an agency may be unmanageable for you! You want an agency that will work with you no matter what your situation.

10. *What happens if some of my creditors will not participate with you?* Some agencies will only accept accounts from creditors who will make a contribution to them for handling your account. A good counseling agency will help with all your debts, regardless of whether the creditor contributes. (Keep in mind that the counseling agency won't be able to negotiate better terms unless the creditor agrees. But it should include the debt in the total monthly payment as a courtesy to you.)

11. *Is there a mandatory upfront fee? How much is it?* Some agencies charge mandatory upfront fees — $250 or more. That's a lot of money for someone who is having trouble paying their current bills.

12. *Will you sell my name or address to outside parties?* Your information should always be kept confidential between you, the agency, and your creditors.

13. *How often do you pay creditors?* This is a critical question. The faster the agency pays creditors, the faster your payment will be credited.

Slow payments by the agency can mean late fees or higher interest for you.

14. *Who will help me if there is a problem with my accounts or creditors?* If problems arise, you want to know the agency will help resolve them.

For more information on choosing a debt counseling agency, and for warnings about other types of credit-related scams, visit:

www.myvesta.org

## Debtors Anonymous

For some people, a support group where they can meet regularly with others who are trying to get out of debt can prove very helpful. Debtors Anonymous (DA) operates such a group. It uses the same underlying principles as Alcoholics Anonymous (AA). To find out if there are DA meetings in your area, or to start one, contact:

**Debtors Anonymous,** P.O. Box 920888, Needham, MA 02492-0009. Phone: 781-453-2743. Web site: www.debtorsanonymous.org.

If you would prefer to read about this approach, we recommend *How to Get Out of Debt, Stay Out of Debt & Live Prosperously,* by Jerrold Mundis.

"It is the greatest of all mistakes to do
nothing because you can only do a little.
Do what you can."

– Sydney Smith

# CHAPTER 7

# The More You Pay, the Less It Costs

D ebt consolidation is not simply a matter of getting a loan at a lower interest rate. It's about taking control of your credit, creating a plan to pay down your debts, and making choices that will enable you to secure your financial future. The first step toward taking this broader view of consolidating your debts is to take the time to figure out exactly how much you owe.

You can use a software program or just sit down with a piece of paper and a pen. Write down the following information for all your loans: your current balance, the interest rate, and the current monthly payment. (Check with your lender if you aren't sure about any of these details.) If you know how long it will take you to pay off the balance, great. If not, use Table #4 on page 16 to estimate how long it will take you to pay off your balances at current rates.

Once you have this information, and you have digested the information we've shared with you about the pros and cons of possible consolidation loans, you can decide whether a new loan will help. Or if your credit report keeps getting in the way of your obtaining a lower-rate loan, you may decide that you'd be better off to keep paying on the loans you already have. Either way, you can save a bundle if you create a plan for cutting back your debt that "fits" with who you are.

## Pre-Pay Your Debts ... and Save a Fortune!

You don't have to get a consolidation loan to get out of debt and save a lot of money. Sure, it will help a lot if you can get a lower interest rate, but you can still save a lot more than you probably realized, without dramatically changing your lifestyle.

Here's how it works: With virtually any loan, you can send in more than you owe. When you do, you shrink the amount of money you'll need to pay back, and you cut the time you'll be in debt. It's simple, painless, and doesn't require an MBA to figure out. You don't need to follow any particular formula, either. But if you do want to know how to pay your debt back within a certain period of time, use Table #5 on page 20 to help you decide how much you'll need to send in every month. You can also use Table #6 on page 21 to total your savings. That alone may be enough to get you and keep you motivated!

🔑 KEY POINT *The bottom line is this: The more you pre-pay and the sooner you begin, the more you'll save.*

## Here's How to Pre-Pay Any Loan:

**Credit cards:** Just pay more than the minimum due. The more you send in, the more money you'll

| Table #10 | | | |
|---|---|---|---|
| **Pee-Wee Credit Card Pre-Payments** | | | |
| Based on a 17% credit card balance, with a 2% minimum | | | |
| Balance | Pre-Payment (Per Day) | Time Saved (Years) | Interest Saved |
| | 0 | 0 | $ 0 |
| $5,000 | 10¢ | 11 | 2,257 |
| | 25¢ | 19 | 4,148 |
| | $1.00 | 30 | 7,624 |
| | 0 | 0 | 0 |
| $10,000 | 10¢ | 12 | 3,060 |
| | 25¢ | 20 | 5,970 |
| | $1.00 | 35 | 12,615 |
| | 0 | 0 | 0 |
| $15,000 | 10¢ | 12 | 3,545 |
| | 25¢ | 21 | 7,112 |
| | $1.00 | 36 | 16,168 |

*Note:* These amounts were calculated with *The Banker's Secret Credit Card Software.*

SLASH YOUR DEBT: Save Money and Secure Your Future

save and the less interest you'll pay. But don't be discouraged if all you can come up with is pocket change. Even a few extra dollars can mean lots of savings. And the sooner you get your credit card payments in, the more you'll save, because your payments will be credited as soon as they're received.

Table #10 on page 82 shows how much money you can save by making "pee-wee pre-payments" of a dime, a quarter, or a dollar a day on typical credit card bills.

**Mortgages:** You can pre-pay your mortgage by sending in more than your required monthly payment. Most lenders will happily credit your extra payment. Your mortgage coupon may even contain a space for writing down the additional amount you want to go toward the outstanding principal balance on your home loan. If not, simply include a note with your check asking that the extra amount you included be credited toward your principal balance.

For a sense of how powerful mortgage pre-payments are, we've included a pre-payment comparison table for a $100,000, 8%, 30-year loan, where the required monthly payment is $734. (See Table #11.) If not pre-paid, the total interest on this loan would be $164,149. But just $15 a month (50 cents a day) will save over $15,000 in interest.

### Table #11

## The More You Pre-Pay, the More You'll Save

Based on a $100,000 mortgage at 8% for 30 years

| Pre-Pay Per Month | Save | Reduce Term by Years/Months |
|---|---|---|
| $  15 | $ 15,054 | 2/3 |
| 25 | 23,337 | 3/7 |
| 50 | 39,906 | 6/2 |
| 75 | 52,484 | 8/2 |
| 100 | 62,456 | 9/10 |
| 125 | 70,610 | 11/3 |
| 150 | 77,431 | 12/5 |
| 175 | 83,240 | 13/5 |
| 200 | 88,260 | 14/4 |
| 225 | 92,649 | 15/1 |
| 250 | 96,524 | 15/10 |
| 275 | 99,976 | 16/5 |
| 300 | 103,071 | 17/0 |
| 325 | 105,866 | 17/7 |
| 350 | 108,404 | 18/0 |
| 375 | 110,719 | 18/6 |
| 400 | 112,841 | 18/11 |
| 425 | 114,793 | 19/3 |
| 450 | 116,597 | 19/7 |
| 475 | 118,268 | 19/11 |
| 500 | 119,821 | 20/3 |
| 750 | 130,930 | 22/6 |
| 1,000 | 137,506 | 23/11 |
| 1,250 | 141,871 | 24/10 |
| 1,500 | 144,986 | 25/7 |
| 1,750 | 147,322 | 26/1 |
| 2,000 | 149,140 | 26/6 |

*Note:* These amounts were calculated with *The Banker's Secret Loan Software.*

For more information on mortgage pre-payment, get "the bible" on the subject, *The Banker's Secret,* by one of the authors of this book, Marc Eisenson. See page 107 or go to:

www.goodadvicepress.com/tbs2.htm.

**Student loans:** Like credit cards and mortgages, student loans carry no penalty for early payment. You can pay them back as fast as you'd like. Just increase your payment whenever you can, by as much as you can.

**Car loans:** You should be able to pre-pay your car loan without any penalty, but there are some car loans which use the "Rule of 78s" or "Sum of the Digits" and for which there is no benefit to sending in pre-payments.

Fortunately, many states now outlaw these loans. Ask your lender to make sure your car loan is not one of them, and ask how to make sure the extra amount you send in will be credited toward the principal balance.

Certainly, when you shop for car loans from now on, make sure you get what is called a "simple interest loan."

## Let Your Personality Be Your Guide When Paying Back Your Debts.

The system you use to pay back your debts will work best if it matches your personality and helps you stay motivated. Here are some approaches you may want to consider:

**Super-Saver:** *You're committed to getting out of debt as quickly as possible and at the absolute lowest cost.*

You'll want to pay down your highest-interest debt first, with as much as you can "penny pinch" from your budget. Pay the minimums on all your other debts until the one that charges the highest interest rate is paid off. Since the required payments on your other cards will be going down, to save the most, keep your total payment outlay constant by upping the amount you send in on your highest-rate card. Then tackle the one with the next-highest rate, and so on, until your slate is wiped clean.

**Evader:** *You'd rather not have to think about your debts.*

In fact, you'd rather get a root canal than create a financial plan. (A survey by the International Association for Financial Planning discovered that there are plenty of you out there!)

You want to get a consolidation loan so you can make just one payment and then forget about your money troubles. Well, we hate to break the news, but there's no way you can avoid dealing with your debts altogether. (Your desire to avoid them may be why you're having to deal with them in such a painful way now!) But you can make it less painful with a clear written plan that will outline for you month-by-month how much to pay on each debt. You'll probably do well to have your monthly payments automatically deducted from your bank account so you don't have to think about them ... and it'll be more difficult to "evade" your opportunity to get out of debt. You might do best with what we refer to as the Monthly Flat Rate Payoff Plan.

As we've explained previously, as the balance due on a credit card account decreases, the required minimum payment goes down. For example, if you have a $5,000 balance on a card that requires a 2% minimum payment, you'd be expected to send in no less than $100 (2% of $5,000) this month. Next month, you'd have to send in $99.42. Every month after that, the amount you'd have to send in would get smaller and smaller (assuming you don't charge anything else on the card).

With the Monthly Flat Rate Payoff Plan, instead of sending in less and less each month, keep sending in this month's required minimum ($100 in this $5,000 example). Send in that $100 every month from now on, until the debt has been paid off (in seven years and four months, rather than 40 years and two months), and you'll save $7,545.

Since you were able to come up with the $100 this month, it should be no burden to come up with it every month. The effect of this flat monthly payment is to make increasingly larger pre-payments as the months go by. As we've shown, the results can be dramatic!

**Impatient:** *You need to see results quickly to stay motivated.*

You may do well by focusing on one debt at a time — and the faster you can pay it off, the better. Your best bet may be to tackle the loan with the lowest balance first. Pay the minimum on every other bill, but muster every resource you can toward paying your target debt until the balance is zero. Then throw yourself a party (make it potluck) and move on to debt number two.

**Organized:** *You balance your checkbook every month, and even your kitchen junk drawer looks neat.*

You may be a candidate for a more challenging method for paying back your credit card debts: The Bi-Weekly (every 14 days) Payoff Plan.

Warning: This system will save you the most, but you must follow these instructions *exactly,* or you'll end up with late fees and a blemish on your credit report.

While you may see promotional materials about mortgage acceleration programs based on bi-weekly payments, those systems are *not* recommended by us (see page 91). On the other hand, you won't see offers for bi-weekly credit card payment plans. That's because they won't make anyone richer — but you!

While most mortgage lenders only credit payments once a month, credit card companies MUST credit payments when they're received as long as they're sent in properly. So a half payment every two weeks will result in 26 half payments a year, which is the equivalent of 13 monthly payments, not 12. The extra month's worth of payments will all go toward paying off your outstanding balance.

To save the most, pick the credit card bill that carries the highest interest rate, and for heaven's sake, stop charging on that card! Say you owe $5,000 on it, and the interest rate is 17%. Your required payment this month could be anywhere from around $100 to $150 (based on that card's required minimum payment).

Let's assume your card issuer requires a 2% minimum, which means you have to send in $100 this month. Get it in by the due date, and start pinching your pennies.

**Believe it or not, if you send in $50 — half of that $100 — every two weeks, from then on, you'll cut your interest bill by a whopping $8,149. And you'll be debt-free in six years and 14 weeks (cutting almost *34 years* off your payments).**

**It's easy!**

The card companies we interrogated as we were developing this payoff plan all said that their computers will know what to do with your bi-weekly payments. Just make sure you get them in every 14 days to the billing address on the monthly statements the card company sends you.

As for those statements, don't let the due date and minimum payments on them confuse you. (But do verify that there are no unexplained charges or fees.) Send in your checks like clockwork, every two weeks, and don't charge anything else on the card.

Ask your card issuer's customer service representative if there's anything you should know about making your bi-weekly payments. For example, the issuers we called advise that you put your account number on the checks. (We'd rather not have this information floating along as the checks are processed, but the companies say it's necessary if you want your payment credited immediately.)

It'd be a good idea every now and then to make sure that what you think you owe is what the purveyor of plastic thinks you owe. How are you supposed to know? Use our *Banker's Secret Loan Software*, or get us to create a payoff plan for you.* Then call the card's customer service number occasionally, to verify that you're on target.

Remember to get this month's full payment in on time, and those bi-weekly payments in every two weeks, no fail! Afraid you'll forget? Ask the card issuer or your bank to electronically transfer your half payments every 14 days. (Be sure there's enough money in your account.) Some companies provide this service for free, while others charge a fee (forget it!), and then there are some that won't help at all.

Sound easy? It is!

However you decide to pay off your debts, send in even more, as often as you can. The more you pre-pay, and the sooner you do it, the more you'll save, and the freer you'll be.

No matter which payoff system you decide to use, take those cards out of your wallet and put them somewhere difficult to reach for awhile. You don't need the temptation. If you must have a card for "emergencies" (and we're talking true emergencies), choose a charge card that you'll have to pay in full or a debit card that immediately deducts purchases from your bank account.

---

*The Banker's Secret Software ($42.95 including s/h) will make it easy for you to generate as many payoff plans as you'd like. Both Windows and Macintosh versions are available. No computer? We can create a personalized plan that shows you how to pay off any credit card or loan fast ($15.95 including s/h). Send your check to us at: Good Advice Press, P.O. Box 78, Elizaville, NY 12523. We'll send you simple instructions and a form to fill out. Mail it back and we'll rush your payoff plan to you. (Additional plans ordered at the same time are just $4.95 each.)

"*The only sure weapon against bad ideas
is better ideas.*"

– Whitney Griswold

# CHAPTER 8

# Scams, Schemes, & Rip-Offs to Avoid

On your road to paying off debt, you'll encounter plenty of companies offering to "help" you. Unfortunately, many of the offers that are targeted to people with credit problems are just plain rotten deals, and will hurt more than they help.

No matter how desperate you feel, avoid any solution that:

- you don't completely understand;
- will cost you more than your current route; or
- sounds too good to be true.

In this chapter we'll share with you some of the most common deals you'll want to avoid.

**Bill-Paying Services:** *We'll pay your bills for you! Make just one payment to us and save yourself the hassle.*

The promise sounds enticing — and you may at first think you are getting a debt consolidation loan. In fact, all that's happening is that you are adding a middleman between you and your creditors. And if that middleman proves unreliable, you could find yourself in trouble.

Bill-paying companies can be damaging in a couple of ways: First, you'll have to pay a fee to have one of these outfits pay your bills. That means you'll have to pay *more* to pay the same old bills. Secondly, you'll be relying on some organization that you probably don't know much about to make your payments for you *on time*. If they don't, you can bet that you'll be the one who will be responsible for those payments plus any additional fees. Unscrupulous companies may just collect your payments and then disappear, leaving you responsible for the bills they didn't pay and with a negative mark for making late payments, which will stay on your credit report for about seven years. Play it safe and stick to reputable financial institutions or a legitimate non-profit counseling agency that will negotiate a repayment plan with your creditors.

**Advance-Fee Loan Scams:** *Loans for any purpose! Easy qualification — bad credit, no problem!*

If you've had a tough time getting the loan you want, you may be a target for companies hoping to cash in on your frustration. Advertising on the Internet, in the classified sections of newspapers, and even by telephone, these firms promise loans in exchange for an upfront fee of as little as $29 to as much as thousands. Advance-fee loan scams have been named one of the top 10 telemarketing scams by the National Consumers League. Don't fall for them!

These companies often operate outside the boundaries of the law. They may be located overseas, for example, and market to U.S. citizens. Federal law prohibits a telemarketer from guaranteeing that a loan can be arranged in exchange for upfront fees. In fact, the law says you must get the loan at least seven days before the company can ask you for payment. But no matter how the loan is marketed (by phone, mail, or on the Internet), no legitimate lender will charge you a fee for a loan (except for an application or appraisal fee) until you are already approved. If a company tells you that you've been approved but requires a fee before the loan can be "processed," go elsewhere. Legitimate lenders always check credit reports of applicants before approving the loan.

**High-Rate Finance Company Loans:** *A check arrives in the mail offering you the opportunity to cash it and pay off all your debts.*

This could be the answer to your prayers, right? Look carefully before you run to the bank! These loans sometimes carry interest rates of 20% or more. At a rate like that, it will cost you a small fortune and take you a long, long time to pay off your bills. If you can't get a better rate than what you're paying now, there's no sense consolidating.

**Pseudo Bi-Weekly Mortgage Acceleration Programs:** *Someone — maybe even your lender — tries to sell you a "conversion" for the mortgage you already have. You'll be "guaranteed" big savings, plus: "No closing fees!" "No reassessments!" and "No points!"*

But you'll have to fork over anywhere from $195 on up ... upfront. And there'll be a contract for you to sign, agreeing to the automatic transfer of loan payments from your bank account to theirs, every two weeks. Then every two weeks, for the next 20 years or so, you'll pay a service charge.

Although the pseudo bi-weekly providers electronically transfer funds every two weeks from your bank account, *they simply send the bank your required mortgage payment once a month* — just as you always did — and in our opinion, ought to continue doing.

Then once or twice a year, the excess that accumulates from your bi-weekly payments will also be sent in. The pseudo-sellers get to collect interest on your money in the meantime.

While they claim to offer something special, the truth is: Everyone can easily save more without outside help, and without all those fees and charges. If your bank won't credit your payment every two weeks

— and most won't — there's no benefit in your sending in bi-weekly payments.

---

## Real Bi-Weekly Mortgages

Real bi-weeklies require one half of a 30-year loan's monthly payment every two weeks, and the lenders really do credit your account every two weeks. That adds up to 26 half payments a year, the equivalent of 13 monthly payments, not 12.

All of that extra month's mortgage payment gets applied to the loan's outstanding balance, which can take about eight years off the term of a standard 30-year loan, and in the process, slash 30% off the loan's interest costs.

There are a few problems with real bi-weeklies: They're rarely available. When they are, you have to take out a brand-new mortgage, which might have expensive closing costs. And you'll have to let the lender automatically deduct those payments every two weeks, which deprives you of even a day of flexibility if times get tough.

---

### The Way to Save More

For greater savings than you can get from a pseudo bi-weekly, divide your current monthly mortgage payment by 12, and send in that amount as a pre-payment with each month's check. Say your mortgage is $125,000 at 7.75% for 30 years, and your required monthly payment is $896. Divide that $896 by 12, and you get $75. Add $75 every month to your mortgage check, and because your pre-payments would be deducted from your balance sooner, you'd save even more than you would with any pseudo. Plus you'd keep the $195 to $400 upfront, there would be no additional bi-weekly fees, and you'd collect extra interest until your check clears the bank.

*Important tip:* If you owe money on credit cards or anything else at a higher interest rate than your mortgage, you'd save the most money by paying those more expensive debts first. However, for many people there's nothing that equals the security of knowing that they own their home free and clear. If that's how you feel, you could put part of your pre-payment dollars toward your home loan and the rest toward your credit card bills.

Just like "there's a sucker born every minute" (according to P. T. Barnum), there's a new scam out there every day. Don't fall victim. Check in from time to time at the following Web sites to stay on top of the latest consumer rip-offs:

www.bbb.org
www.fraud.org
www.consumer.gov

"No one knows what he can do till he tries."

– Publilius Syrus

# CHAPTER 9

# Strategies for Success

F or most of us, budgeting is a chore. But if you really want to get out of debt and stay there, creating a spending plan and sticking to it is essential. The first step in developing a budget is to find out where your money goes. You think you know? If you haven't kept careful track, you're probably in for a big surprise.

Karen Varcoe, a consumer economics management specialist at the University of California, Riverside Extension, tells the story of one client she worked with who tracked his spending and discovered he was blowing $160 a week in vending machines! And at one of Gerri's seminars, a participant piped up and said she was shocked to learn that her family was forking out $120 for pizza delivery each month.

## Where's Your Money Really Going?

To find out, write down every single penny you and your family spend — yes, every last penny, nickel, and dime — for at least 30 days.

Don't drive yourself and your family nuts, just keep up with it the best you can. The family that works together, saves together.

*Tip:* Great tools for tracking your spending include the Montguide, a specially designed checkbook register, available for $1 from Montana State University, Extension Publications Office, Check Register, Bozeman, MT 59717. We also recommend *The Money Tracker* and *The Budget Kit* by Judy Lawrence.

Once you've collected information about your spending, you can create your budget. Be gentle with yourself! Cut back where it will be painless, but don't be unrealistically drastic. For example, you might try to shave $5 a week, or even $5 a month, off one spending category, and then keep cutting in that area by $5 until you reach a level you can live with, perhaps without some frills, but with no discomfort, either. No budget will work if it leaves you feeling deprived!

Keep in mind that the reason you are tracking your spending and creating a budget is so you can free up funds to pay down your debts faster, and to keep out of frivolous debt in the future. To do this, you'll have to find a way to make sure that the money you save goes toward paying down your current bills. You might want to set aside a jar where you stash whatever cash you can save. At the end of the month, deposit the cash and write a check toward one of your bills. Don't "borrow" from it in the meantime. Remember: Your family's future is at stake!

If you have a spouse or children, budget together. Younger kids can handle general discussions about "needs" versus "wants," and can help with little money-saving projects like turning off lights when they leave a room. Older kids can understand budgets and learn to live within an allowance you set together. You don't have to scare them with your tales of how broke you are. Let them share in the fact that you are going through a tough time, but that you are also taking control and doing something positive about it. Point out that other families who seem to "have everything" may also have a lot of debt or too little in savings.

A great resource for learning how to change your spending habits and stop fighting about money is money therapist Olivia Mellan's book, *Overcoming Overspending*.

## Seven Steps to Staying Motivated

You may start out on your debt-reduction plan with the best of intentions and plenty of excitement. But sticking with it is another thing altogether. Try these strategies for getting and staying motivated:

## 1. Set both short-term and long-term goals.

If your get-out-of-debt plan will take five years (which is not unusual these days), you'll need some shorter-term goals to celebrate. It may mean paying off a small bill first, or reaching a certain balance on an account. Reach a goal and reward yourself — inexpensively, of course!

## 2. Set your sights high.

Create realistic goals that require you to stretch beyond your usual "comfort zone." For you, it may be getting through one day without spending any money at all. Or it may be cutting your clothing budget in half until your debts are paid. If reaching the goal doesn't cause you any discomfort, it's probably too easy. But if it's too difficult, it won't work. Try to strike a healthy balance.

## 3. Stay in control.

Remind yourself frequently why you're trying to get out of debt: to have more money for funding your important goals, like a college education for your kids, and to create a more secure financial future, including a carefree retirement. Think about how much more money you'll have when those debts are paid, and decide how you'd like to spend, or better yet, invest it.

## 4. State your intentions.

Make a commitment to pay off your debts, and tell someone, perhaps a supportive friend or a relative. Avoid discussing your situation with people who won't support you, or who may feel threatened by your efforts. And please write to us at Good Advice Press, (P.O. Box 78, Elizaville, NY 12523), to share your goals and experiences along the way to debt-free living.
(Or send us an e-mail — feedback@goodadvicepress.com.)

## 5. Stay on top of it.

Pay careful attention to where you're spending your money, and how you're progressing toward your goals. Consider creating a chart you can post where you'll see it often. Track your spending from time to time to make sure you're still on course. It's the little things that will get away from you. Those trickles of spending may well turn into a flood, so plug the dike early.

## 6. Give yourself a break.

Nobody's perfect. Life will get in the way of your plans from time to time, and financial emergencies will crop up. When setbacks occur, feel free to complain for a day. Then get yourself back on track as soon as you can. This is a long-term commitment you're making — keep your perspective.

## 7. Get support.

There's nothing wrong with asking for help. A friend or relative can become your "budget buddy," who monitors your progress and helps you stay on track. You may want to join an organization like Debtors Anonymous (see page 79), or get help from a minister or a counseling agency like Myvesta (formerly Debt Counselors of America) (see page 76).

### Q & A

Q: **I love to shop! Whenever I'm bored or upset, I head to the mall. It makes me feel better. I just don't see how I can change.**

A: If you're a chronic overspender, first get a dose of reality. A visit to a meeting of Debtors Anonymous (see page 79) may be just what you need to see where your spending habits are likely to lead. If that's not your cup of tea, you must find another diversion for your time. (This is not optional!) Get involved in a new hobby or an activity you've been putting off. Choose a good cause and volunteer. Helping others less fortunate than yourself may be an excellent way to take your mind off your troubles, fill your free time, and even make some new and lasting friendships. Don't know where to volunteer? Ask at your place of worship, contact your local United Way for ideas, or call your mayor's office to see if your community has a volunteer center. You can also find lots of volunteer information online at:

www.idealist.org and www.change.net

If you simply can't break the shopping habit, leave your credit cards at home and start a shopping service for others or develop another small business. You could even take a part-time job at the mall. If you do, enjoy the employee discounts, but don't spend your whole paycheck there!

**Q: I am considering a loan that has low monthly payments for three years, but then I have to pay it off in full. I figure by that time, I'll be making more money and have my credit under control. What do you think?**

A: Stay away from loans like this with what are called "balloon" payments (low monthly payments with a large chunk due at the end) — unless you are certain you'll be receiving a large enough windfall to pay off the loan when the balance comes due, and you're sure you can trust yourself to use it wisely. You probably can't predict with great certainty what will happen to you financially in the next three years. Nor can you be sure that you will be able to get another loan should you need it to pay off the balloon. See if you can swing a more typical three-year (or, at least, a five-year) loan instead, so that you'll be making your last payment in that time frame, instead of starting to worry all over again about how to pay off that balance.

**Q: I was asked for my Social Security number while shopping for a consolidation loan. Does that mean the bank ran a credit check?**

A: Yes. If you are shopping around for a consolidation loan or any other kind of loan, don't give out your Social Security number unless you've decided to actually fill out an application. Some lenders will run a credit check just to quote a rate — and that results in an inquiry on your credit report. More than a few inquiries on your report in a six-month period can hurt your chances of getting the loan you want, so be careful.

**Q: What happens to my credit when my consolidation loan is finally paid?**

A: First, you'll have every reason to celebrate! You'll definitely have earned it. When you use a consolidation loan to pay off a loan or credit card, ask the lender to close the account and report to the credit bureaus that the account has been closed. (They are required to report your account as "closed at your request," if you ask them to do so.) This can bolster your credit rating. In the end, having a couple of credit cards that you use wisely will probably be more than enough. And having paid off all that debt will definitely help your credit, not to mention your bottom line!

## Final Thoughts ...

Congratulations! If you've read this far, you're certainly seriously interested in consolidating your debts, saving money, and building a solid financial foundation for your family. Now all you have to do is: DO it! Stop charging, start consolidating, keep paying off your bills, and watch your spending. The money you save and the future you create will truly be your own.

Please let us know how you're doing! You can write to us in care of Good Advice Press, the small business we started in 1984 to help people get out of debt, save money, and live better on less. (Good Advice Press, P.O. Box 78, Elizaville, NY 12523, www.goodadvicepress.com, feedback@goodadvicepress.com.)

Gerri, Marc, & Nancy

P.S. For other great tools we think will help you succeed at intelligently managing your money and creating a lifestyle that you will enjoy and be able to afford, see pages 103 – 108.

# Author Biographies

**Gerri Detweiler** is education advisor to the nonprofit Myvesta (formerly Debt Counselors of America) (www.myvesta.org) and former executive director of the nonprofit consumer education and advocacy group, Bankcard Holders of America. She is author of *The Ultimate Credit Handbook* (Plume, 1993, revised 1997). *The Ultimate Credit Handbook* was featured in *Money* magazine as one of the five best new personal finance books of the year when it was released in 1993.

More recently, with Marc Eisenson and Nancy Castleman, Gerri co-authored *Invest in Yourself: Six Secrets to a Rich Life* (Wiley, 1998), which has been highly praised by personal finance writers from coast to coast. The book lays out practical strategies for setting priorities (like spending more time with your family), going after your goals (like funding your retirement), and getting the most for your money (whether you want to drive a new Lexus or a used VW Bug).

Gerri has written articles for publications including *Woman's Day* magazine and *Bottom Line Personal*, and has been quoted in numerous national publications including *The New York Times*, *USA Today*, *The Wall Street Journal*, and *The Washington Post*. She has co-hosted an award-winning syndicated financial radio program, and has also been a guest on network television programs including The Today Show, Dateline NBC, CBS Evening News, and CNN. Gerri has spoken to over a hundred audiences across the country and internationally.

She has also developed educational materials and programs for organizations such as Union Privilege, AFL-CIO, and the Financial Literacy Center. She has served on the Board of Directors of the National Coalition for Consumer Education and on Experian's Consumer Advisory Council, and is currently an active member of the National Capital Speakers Association and Toastmasters.

Gerri holds a B.A. in International Business/Political Affairs from Taylor University and an M.A. in Adult Education/Psychology (with a focus on financial education) from Vermont College at Norwich University.

**Marc Eisenson,** author of the bestseller *The Banker's Secret,* is known as the expert on how to painlessly exit from debt, and is widely regarded as one of the foremost financial thinkers of our time. With his partner **Nancy Castleman,** Marc has spent the last 17 years teaching Americans the secrets to saving money, managing debts, and living better on less. Through books, software, audiotapes, and an assortment of other publications, their small, home-based consumer advocacy business, Good Advice Press, has saved hundreds of thousands of families billions of dollars.

Marc and Nancy originally self-published *The Banker's Secret,* which has been dubbed by the media as the bible of mortgage pre-payment. It was greatly expanded over the years, and was subsequently published by Villard, a division of Random House. The pair continue to distribute it to this day from the old farmhouse where they live and work in upstate New York. Over the years, they've created (and upgraded) companion software that makes it easy to save money on mortgages as well as credit cards and other loans.

Since 1990, Marc and Nancy have also published the highly respected *Pocket Change Investor* newsletter, which helps consumers make savvy financial choices on subjects like refinancing, taxes, and credit cards. They also help readers to tackle difficult lifestyle decisions, and have been championing the value of a debt-free, simple life since 1984 — long before "downsizing debt," "voluntary simplicity," and "tightwaddery" were politically correct.

Hundreds of reporters, producers, and editors across the nation receive, ingest, and report on their often provocative, but always well-documented, sound advice. Marc speaks to members of the media every day, and they regularly showcase his ideas on radio and television, in virtually every newspaper, as well as in every personal finance, business, and women's magazine.

Marc Eisenson and Nancy Castleman are also co-authors with Gerri Detweiler of *Invest in Yourself: Six Secrets to a Rich Life* (Wiley, 1998), which shows ways to invest your time, money, and energy for great payoffs in life.

# Bibliography

Bamford, Janet. *Smarter Insurance Solutions*. Princeton: Bloomberg, 1996.

Burkett, Larry. *Debt-Free Living*. Chicago: Moody Press, 1989.

Cash, Grady. *Spend Yourself Rich*. Kalamazoo: Financial Literacy Center, 1998.

Celente, Gerald. *Trends 2000*. New York: Warner, 1998.

Chatzky, Jean. *The Rich & Famous Money Book*. New York: Wiley, 1999.

Chilton, David. *The Wealthy Barber*. Rocklin, CA: Prima, 1998.

Clason, George S. *The Richest Man in Babylon*. New York: New American Library, 1997.

Daily, Frederick W. *Stand Up to the IRS*. Berkeley: Nolo Press, 1998.

Detweiler, Gerri. *The Ultimate Credit Handbook*. New York: Plume, 1997.

Dolan, Ken and Daria. *Straight Talk on Money*. New York: Simon & Schuster, 1993.

Dominguez, Joe, and Vicki Robin. *Your Money or Your Life*. New York: Penguin, 1993.

Dugas, Christine. *Fiscal Fitness: A Guide to Shaping Up Your Finances for the Rest of Your Life*. Kansas City: Andrews and McMeel, 1995.

Dunnan, Nancy. *Dun & Bradstreet Guide to Your Investments*. New York: Harper Perennial, 1999.

Edelman, Ric. *The Truth About Money*. Washington, DC: Georgetown University, 1996.

Eisenson, Marc. *The Banker's Secret*. New York: Villard Books, 1991.

Eisenson, Marc, and Nancy Castleman. *The Banker's Secret Loan Software*. Elizaville, NY: Good Advice Press, 1997.

Eisenson, Marc, Gerri Detweiler, and Nancy Castleman. *Invest in Yourself: Six Secrets to a Rich Life*. New York: Wiley, 1998.

Elias, S., A. Renauer, and R. Leonard. *How to File for Bankruptcy*. Berkeley: Nolo Press, 1998.

Englander, Debra. *How to Be Your Own Financial Planner*. Rocklin, CA: Prima, 1996.

Feinberg, Andrew. *Downsize Your Debt*. New York: Penguin, 1993.

Green, Mark. *The Consumer Bible*. New York: Workman, 1998.

Howard, Clark, and Mark Meltzer. *Clark Howard's Consumer Survival Kit III*. Marietta, GA: Longstreet Press, 1999.

Jaffe, Charles. *The Right Way to Hire Financial Help*. Cambridge, MA: MIT Press, 1999.

Johnson, Randy. *How to Save Thousands of Dollars on Your Home Mortgage*. New York: Wiley, 1998.

Jorgensen, James. *It's Never Too Late to Get Rich*. New York: Simon & Schuster, 1995.

Kehrer, Daniel. *Kiplinger's 12 Steps to a Worry-Free Retirement*. Washington, DC: Kiplinger Books, 1998.

Kobliner, Beth. *Get a Financial Life*. New York: Fireside, 1996.

Kristof, Kathy. *Kathy Kristof's Complete Book of Dollars and Sense*. New York: Macmillan, 1997.

Lawrence, Judy. *The Budget Kit*. Chicago: Dearborn, 1997.

Lawrence, Judy. *The Money Tracker: A Quick and Easy Way to Keep Tabs on Your Spending*. Chicago: Dearborn, 1996.

Leonard, Robin. *Money Troubles: Legal Strategies to Cope with Your Debts*. Berkeley: Nolo Press, 1997.

Leonard, Robin, and Shae Irving. *Take Control of Your Student Loans*. Berkeley: Nolo Press, 1997.

McCoy, Jonni. *Miserly Moms*. Elkton, MD: Full Quart Press, 1996.

Mellan, Olivia. *Money Harmony*. New York: Walker & Co., 1994.

Mellan, Olivia, with Sherry Christie. *Overcoming Overspending: A Winning Plan for Spenders and Their Partners*. New York: Walker & Co., 1997.

Mrkvicka, Edward F. Jr. *Your Bank is Ripping You Off*. New York: St. Martin's Griffin, 1997.

Mundis, Jerrold. *How to Get Out of Debt, Stay Out of Debt & Live Prosperously*. New York: Bantam Books, 1990.

Pond, Jonathan D. *4 Easy Steps to Successful Investing*. New York: Avon, 1998.

Quinn, Jane Bryant. *Making the Most of Your Money*. New York: Simon & Schuster, 1997.

Reader's Digest. *Back to Basics*. Pleasantville, NY: Reader's Digest Association, 1981.

Richard, Paul. *Do-It-Yourself Credit File Correction Guide*. San Diego: NCFE, 1998.

Roberts, William. *How to Save Money on Just About Everything*. Boulder, CO: Paladin Press, 1993.

Roth, Larry. *The Simple Life*. New York: Berkley, 1998.

Rowland, Mary. *The New Commonsense Guide to Mutual Funds*. Princeton: Bloomberg Press, 1998.

Stanley, Thomas J., and William D. Danko. *The Millionaire Next Door*. New York: Pocket Books, 1998.

Stevens, James Talmage. *Making the Best of Basics*. Seattle: Gold Leaf Press, 1997.

Tobias, Andrew. *The Only Investment Guide You'll Ever Need*. New York: Harcourt Brace, 1998.

Warner, Ralph. *Get a Life: You Don't Need a Million to Retire Well*. Berkeley: Nolo Press, 1998.

Woodhouse, Violet, and Victoria F. Collins. *Divorce and Money*. Berkeley: Nolo Press, 1998.

## Authors' Recommended Products

## Books

These resources are available through Good Advice Press, P.O. Box 78, Elizaville, NY 12523, www.goodadvicepress.com.

### Invest in Yourself: Six Secrets to a Rich Life — Marc Eisenson, Gerri Detweiler, and Nancy Castleman

A truly rich life is one that lets you live where you want and have what you want — with enough money to satisfy your needs and secure your future. Invest in this book, written by Marc Eisenson, Gerri Detweiler, and Nancy Castleman, and you'll be well on your way, going beyond getting your debts under control to creating the life you want.

**ISBN #0-471-24888-6 • Hardcover • 326 pages**

### The Ultimate Credit Handbook — Gerri Detweiler

Too much debt? Damaged credit rating? No credit? Let Gerri Detweiler show you how to solve your credit problems and take control of your debt in this comprehensive, no-nonsense guide. Named one of the five best new personal finance books of the year in *Money* magazine! Now available in a new, updated edition that explains the latest credit laws.

**ISBN #0-452-27712-4 • Paperback • 292 pages**

### The Banker's Secret — Marc Eisenson

Marc Eisenson shows you how to save literally thousands of dollars, using just your pocket change to pay off your mortgage, credit cards, and other debts. You'll get complete step-by-step instructions, plus lots of easy-to-use tables that will show you exactly how much you'll save. You'll be amazed, inspired — and on your way to debt-free living!

**ISBN #0-394-58604-2 • Hardcover • 232 pages**

*more ...*

# Spend Yourself Rich — Grady Cash, CFP

Published by the Financial Literacy Center

Spend yourself rich is an enticing promise — wouldn't we all like to spend our way to wealth? But Grady Cash isn't making an empty promise, or serving up a get-rich-quick scheme. You'll discover we're all different when it comes to spending money. We have individual "spending personalities." Cash will help you identify your unique personality and then show you how to use it to save money, conquer debt, and build wealth.

**ISBN #0-9659638-2-9 • Paperback • 107 pages**

# The Peanut Butter and Jelly Game — Adam Eisenson

Don't let your kids or grandkids learn about money the way you did — the hard way! Give them a great head start with this beautifully illustrated picture book that teaches children in grades K-3 about smart spending. Great message, fun story, wonderful gift.

**ISBN #0-943973-16-3 • Hardcover • 32 pages**

**Audiotape**

# Smart Credit Strategies for College Students — Gerri Detweiler

This important audiotape helps teens use credit wisely, avoid its pitfalls, and cut through the card issuers' hype. Gerri Detweiler shares her money-saving advice on choosing and using credit cards — in language teens understand. Ask yours to pop the cassette into their headset for the lowdown on managing credit. It won't feel like another homework assignment.

**ISBN #0-943973-18-X • 1 Cassette/30 minutes**